Althusser and Feminism

Althusser and Feminism

Alison Assiter

PLUTO  PRESS

London • Winchester Mass

First published 1990 by Pluto Press
345 Archway Road, London N6 5AA
and 8 Winchester Place, Winchester
01890 MA, USA

British Library Cataloguing in Publication Data
Assiter, Alison
  Althusser and feminism
  1. Feminism. Theories of Althusser, Louis
  I. Title
  305.4′2′01

  ISBN 0-7453-0294-7

Library of Congress Cataloging-in-Publication Data
Assiter, Alison.
  Althusser and feminism / Alison Assiter.
     p.   cm.
  Includes bibliographical references.
  ISBN 0-7453-0294-7
  1. Althusser, Louis. 2. Feminism–History–20th century.
I. Title.
B2430.A474A86 1990
305.4–dc20   89-70911
                                                         CIP

Typeset by Fine Line Publishing Services, Witney
Printed in Great Britain by Billing and Sons Ltd, Worcester

Contents

Introduction

In this 'post-structuralist', 'post-feminist' era, many expressions have become common intellectual currency. Some of them have positive connotations, whilst others carry more negative overtones. Amongst the expressions in question are 'structuralist', which can be said about someone/something in a positive vein, though the thinker/body of ideas/'text' is better still if they can be classified as a structuralist of the 'post' variety. 'Plurality', and being 'decentred' are further terms that carry positive connotations. Terms, on the other hand, that are generally viewed negatively in the genre are 'economism', 'positivism', empiricism', 'liberal humanism' and 'individualism'.

It was structuralists themselves who began valorising some of the above terms and debasing the others. The structuralist intellectual current is associated predominantly with the work of Louis Althusser and Claude Lévi-Strauss. For those schooled in the 'post-structuralist' thought of Jacques Derrida, Jacques Lacan and others (the label 'post' is used although Althusser was, in fact, influenced by Lacan), Louis Althusser himself falls foul of many of the objectionable tendencies he noticed in Hegel, the empiricists and the early Marx. He himself is too 'posituristic' in his thinking, too empiricist, too much of a humanist.

Louis Althusser's work represented an attempt to re-theorise Marx's historical (and dialectical, he would have said) materialism in such a fashion as to free Marx from the economistic, empiricist errors that were latent in his writings. He wanted to present us with a Marx 'purged' of economism, humanism, historicism etc.

I argue in this book that, *contra* Althusser, Marx was an economistic thinker, and also that he was a humanist of a sort. 'Economism' is a term that has taken on many different senses in the literature and, although Marx's thought does not fit all interpretations of the term, it can be classified as economistic, on many readings of the expression. 'Humanism', too, has different senses. There is one interpretation of the term – namely that the individual pre-exists language, the production process and other such systems – that I argue refers to a position which is true, and which Marx, again *contra* Althusser, upheld. Marx does not believe, Althusser notwithstanding, that individuals are created in the production process. Nor is it true that individuals come into being in such a fashion.

Against one reading of Lacan, too, I argue that individuals pre-exist language: they are not 'created' in language. But there is another claim that is associated with humanism, that derives from Descartes. It holds that individuals are whole, non-fragmented beings, fully self-conscious, and that they gain this self-consciousness by means of self-reflection. This I dispute in the book. (This is not a claim, I believe, that concerned Marx, so I do not spend time attributing either view to him.)

Finally, 'structuralism': here I argue – and this is where the book begins – that 'structuralism' is not a useful or a helpful term when it comes to understanding Marx. On some interpretations of the term, where Althusser is a structuralist, he cannot be said to be a follower of Marx.

My overall view of Althusser and structuralism, then, as far as Marxism and some aspects of 'the truth' are concerned, is negative. Structuralism does not help us understand historical materialism; Marx is an 'economistic', in fact a 'technological determinist' thinker, and he is a humanist on one issue at least: he believes that people are natural, biological beings.

On the other hand, I argue that Althusser does have something helpful to offer us as far as feminism is concerned. Feminist critiques of 'economistic' Marxism have become commonplace, and I rehearse some of the arguments in the book. On the other hand, socialist feminist criticism of 'radical feminism' is almost as familiar. I run through some of these criticisms too. An appropriate feminism, that does not fall foul of the two sets of objections can, I argue, be developed, drawing on Althusser's writings on ideology. My reading of Althusser here, however, is akin to his own readings of Marx – it is more faithful to the 'spirit' than to the letter of his writings. The 'oppression of women', I suggest, is not simply an ideological phenomenon. The analysis I offer of women's oppression is compatible with economistic Marxism.

In the course of my discussion, I digress a little to consider the work of a representative 'post-structuralist' French feminist, Luce Irigaray, whose work has often been classified, by Anglo-American feminists, as 'essentialist', and as subject to the same criticisms as the radical feminists mentioned earlier. I suggest that, although some of the same criticisms do apply, one must not reach this conclusion too quickly, and one must understand the Derridean Lacanian influences on her work.

Overall, then, as far as the 'structuralism' of Louis Althusser is concerned, I argue that it has little to offer us as Marxists, but much to give us as feminists.

1
Althusser and Structuralism

The writings of Louis Althusser are taken to be exemplary if not paradigmatic of structuralism, even though he himself dissents from applying the label to his work: 'We believe that despite the terminological ambiguity, the profound tendency of our texts was not attached to the "structuralist" ideology.'[1]

In what is probably the most wide-ranging discussion of Althusser's thought to date, Gregory Elliott has this to say on the subject: 'Perceiving a convergence between the astringent anti-humanism of structuralism and his own Marxist positions, Althusser informed the Italian Communist newspaper *Rinascita* in 1964 that Lévi-Strauss was more of an immediate ally of historical materialism than Sartre. Quite the reverse of the mere "flirt" with structuralist terminology to which he reduced this episode in his later autocritique, Althusser's Theoriepolitik dictated something aproaching what Nicos Poulantzas would describe as an alliance with "structuralism against historicism, Lévi-Strauss against Sartre".'[2] In this chapter, I shall present a distilled version of some of the themes that are common to those who are given the label 'structuralist' and discuss some of the respects in which Althusser fits the bill. I shall argue further that there is a tension between Althusser's structuralism and his Marxism.

The Background

In the literature, one finds a number of different definitions of structuralism. Many of these would probably be denounced by those who might, for other reasons, wish to call themselves 'structuralist'. There are structuralist theories in mathematical logic, philosophy of science,[3] in biology, in anthropology, in linguistics, in sociology.

Piaget suggests that 'structuralism' has slightly different senses in each of these various areas. He describes it generally as a theory that deals in self-sufficient and self-regulating wholes. In mathematics, it is opposed to 'compartmentalism' – it deals in wholes rather than in isolated elements; in linguistics, it represents a departure from diachronic studies of isolated linguistic phenomena to a synchronic study of unified linguistic systems (in other words, it moves from research into the variation in linguistic units over time to a comparative analysis of different languages at any one point in time). In psychology, structuralism is contrasted with atomism; and in philosophy it is opposed to historicism.

The variety in types of structuralism and in areas of its application has caused A.L. Kroeber to say this: '"Structure" appears to be just yielding to a word that has a perfectly good meaning but suddenly becomes fashionably attractive ... everything that is not wholly amorphous has a structure ... what "structure" adds to the meaning of our phrase seems to be nothing, except to provide a degree of pleasant puzzlement.'

Miriam Glucksmann derives the word 'structure' from the Latin 'structura' from 'struere': to construct.[5] According to her: 'Its meaning was exclusively architectural until the seventeenth century when its use was extended to the study of anatomy and grammar ... The arrangement of the organs of the body came to be viewed as a kind of construction, and language was understood as the arrangement of words in speech having a "structured" character.'[6] In the nineteenth century, she tells us, the term was introduced from biology to the new 'sciences of man' by Herbert Spencer.

Originally then the term referred to a property of something or the way something is constructed. A structure was an abstract property of something else; something possessed by something else. And for what it is worth, this sense accords with some contemporary English usage – buildings have structure, arguments have a structure. One could not have an argument or a building without a structure: their structures are part of what makes them buildings or arguments. On the other hand, the building or the argument is not to be identified with its structure – without a structure there is no building but the building and its structure are not one and the same. They are both instantiated in the same object; one is a property of the other. Structure, however, is not attached to particular things in the way that, say, being made up of a collection of bricks is a property of a particular house. Get rid of all the bricks and you have destroyed the house, but replacing the bricks and rebuilding the house leaves the structure of the building intact.

Whatever else an analysis of a random selection of cases might reveal about structure, it tells us this: structure seems not to be a thing in its own right. A. Schaff shares this view. According to him, originally a structure was a structure of something: 'The way those elements are interconnected within a given system, i.e. the totality of the relations among them, is termed a structure of that system.'[7] A system was 'a whole consisting of elements bearing such a relation to one another that a change in the position of one results in a change in the position of the rest.'[8] There could be no structure without a system and vice versa. Schaff informs us that de Saussure, according to many one of the main structuralists, did not use the term 'structure' at all, but only system. A system, then, is a kind of entity – an abstract entity – and a structure is one of its properties. The task, for some scientists, is to uncover the structure of a system.

But Schaff goes on to say that 'structure' is also used to mean 'system': something which has a specified structure. This usage, indeed, is common amongst recent structuralists, particularly those in the French school (see Lévi-Strauss, Barthes and Althusser himself) and also amongst commentators on this school and others.[9] This usage, has become commonplace in the literature. So there is a quite specific ambiguity in the meaning of the term.

There may not be any set of features which all 'structuralists' would uphold, but is there a collection of views which would entitle us to put them all together in a school? A. Schaff lists the following four characteristics which form, he suggests, an intellectual trend: first, structuralists approach the subject matter of their research as a specific whole which dominates all its elements. They are critical of atomism, where things are studied as discrete parts of an aggregate, and where wholes are no more than the sum of their parts. The whole, according to the structuralist, forms a system the elements of which are interconnected and where the structure of the whole determines the position of each element. Secondly, structuralists believe that every system has a structure: the task of science is to find out what the structure is. And thirdly, structuralists are interested in 'morphological' or 'structural' laws. The laws deal not in changes but with coexistence. They therefore tend towards having a static approach to facts. And, finally, most structuralists would not deny that the dynamic or the diachronic is important in science, but they would say that this is wholly complementary to synchronic analysis.

Those are four features listed by Schaff. There is a fifth we might mention, one which figures in C. Sumner as the defining feature of structuralism, and that is to see 'structures' as the real things which underlie the appearances, and which are usually opaque to the eye. Sumner: 'Structuralism is a method which examines phenomena as the outward expressions of their inner, invisible structures.'[10] And for this feature see also Keat and Urry.[11]

Let us see how these properties of structuralism are exemplified in those who apply the label to their work. The first feature of structuralism appears in Saussure's description of the function of language. Language he characterises as a system of signs.[12] Collections of noises count as language only when they serve to express or communicate ideas; and to communicate ideas, they must be part of a system of conventions: a system of signs. A sign is a union of a 'form which signifies' – a signifier – and the idea signified. (Philosophers might label these, respectively, the word and the concept. They might, however, say that, as it stands, Saussure's claim does not distinguish the 'referent' of the sign – what it picks out – from its sense; what Frege described as the 'mode of presentation' of the sign.)[13] The linguistic sign, for Saussure, is arbitrary: there is no natural link between the signifier and the signified. There is no link, for instance, between the sound of the sign and its signification, and signs change their meanings – for instance, a 'silly' person was once happy, blessed and pious.

Signifiers are not autonomous, but they are defined by their relations with other members of the system. What gives the word 'brown' its identity is not anything intrinsic to it, but its difference from other colour words. The identity of the sign consists in its place in the system of signifiers.

The first of the outlined features of structuralism is apparent in Levi-Strauss, who perceives ceremonies, rites, methods of cooking not as discrete entities but in terms of the contrastive relations they bear to each other. 'Like phonemes, kinship terms are elements of meaning; like phonemes, they acquire meaning only if they are integrated into systems.'[14] Kinship terms for him *are of the same type* as linguistic phenomena'.[15] (Lévi-Strauss's italics) Each system – kinship, food etc. contains a partial expression of the total culture.

The fifth feature is apparent too in Lévi-Strauss. According to him, we are to use structural linguistics, which moves from conscious linguistic phenomena to their unconscious infrastructure, in the study of kinship systems.

This fifth feature appears in de Saussure as a distinction between *la langue* – the system of linguistic signs underlying everyday speech patterns, and the latter. 'We must take *la langue* as our point of departure and use *langue* as the norm of all other manifestations of language.[16] This feature appears also in Barthes. Examples in Barthes lie in the 'garment' system and in the 'food' system. In Barthes' semiology, food is not just that but is also a system of signs which signify.[17] Within this system, according to Barthes, one can find de Saussure's *langue*. It is made of '(i) rules of exclusion (alimentary taboos); (ii) signifying oppositions of units, the type of which remains to be determined (for instance, the type *savoury/sweet*); (iii) rules of association, either simultaneous (at the level of a dish) or successive at the level of the menu etc.'[18] (Barthes' italics) One finds also, within the system, de Saussure's 'parole'. So the menu, for Barthes, is a kind of language, and has meaning as sentences do. The meaning of a menu has to be 'read' from various menus. And here we uncover another feature of some structuralisms, particularly semiological ones: the way in which the 'real essence' is uncovered from an acquaintance with the 'appearance'. For Barthes, a menu, or a system of clothing has a 'code of significance' like a language has a grammar. The menu has a structure determining the nature of possible menus. This structure of the menu may not be transparently recoverable from actual menus; for they present the structure only partially, or opaquely. As in the hermeneutic tradition, one may have to reconstruct structures of systems from only partial evidence.[19]

We have uncovered five features common to most structuralisms and a sixth which appears particularly in semiological structuralism. In the latter the analogy between language and other 'sign systems' is taken to be important. For Barthes, menus, car systems, furniture systems[20] have meaning just as languages do.

Before proceeding to discuss Althusser's structuralism, I should just like to mention a few criticisms one might level against structuralism as so far presented.

Criticisms

De Saussure, for instance, emphasises that elements in a language should be combined but it could be said to be a failing that he does not offer detailed remarks on the way in which this combination is to be effected: on the way in which individual words combine to form sentences and the manner in which sentences form languages. More recent linguists and logicians, for example Chomsky and D. Davidson have stressed the importance of rules governing the combination of units in a language and have offered detailed accounts of the way the rules work.

A more detailed criticism might be presented of those structuralists – the semiologists – who extend the idea of a sign system outside the realm of language. Saussure himself envisaged this extension of his thinking. He said: '*A science that studies the life of signs within society* is conceivable; it would be a part of social psychology ... I shall call it *semiology* (from Greek semeion 'sign')[21] In the work of Lévi-Strauss, as we have seen, anthropology came to be seen as a branch of semiology; and with Barthes all sorts of aspects of reality – traffic light systems, furniture systems, menus etc. are seen as having meaning in the way that languages do. They are said to have structure and are supposed to be able to be used to convey information of some kind. But it is a little difficult to see how the analogy can work. Whatever structure a menu has is without semantic import. A menu does not have a grammar: it does not have a way of determining the contribution of the meanings of the parts to the meaning of the whole. And hence there can be no way of determining whether or not unactualised menus are legitimate according to the structure. The problem of how it is that a person can produce infinitely many sentences on the basis of knowledge of a finite number of parts is one that occupied Chomsky and also Davidson.[22] In other words, they were concerned to show how a knowledge of the 'structure' of language – for Chomsky the rules of syntax, innate in the mind, and for Davidson a knowledge of the meanings of the parts of a language together with an understanding of the 'logical' rules building up wholes from parts – yields the possibility of distinguishing meaningful from meaningless unuttered sentences. But there can be no such procedure in the case of a menu. Any proposed structure is arbitrary in a stronger than Saussurean sense; it is not limited as is language by the constraint of the possibility of communication. Some unuttered sentences must be ruled out on the grounds that they have no semantic import; ultimately they cannot be used to say anything. But, though some meals may be ruled out as inedible, this will not be because of the structure of any menu. A menu may have a perfectly acceptable structure and the meal still be inedible; alternatively the menu may appear to have no acceptable structure at all yet the meal could be very tasty.

It appears, then, that there are difficulties with some sorts of structuralism, and particularly with those of the semiological variety. I propose now to go on to discuss Althusser and structuralism.

Althusser and Structuralism

Althusser upholds enough of the theses I have identified to be labelled a 'structuralist'. He dislikes empiricism and emphasises 'totalities',[23] the 'structure à dominante'[24] and 'complex wholes'.[25] These entities are not separable from the elements that compose them,[26] nor are they nothing but the sum of their parts – they are elements: relations of production, forces of production etc. connected in specific ways. Indeed the nature of each part of the whole is determined by its role in the totality. Economic practice, for example, does not exist on its own but only as part of the 'complex structure'.

I should like now to describe in more detail the way in which Althusser's 'totality' fits or fails to fit the first outlined feature of structuralism. I shall describe the type of totality of which he is critical; and I shall draw on the ideas of a thinker whom he acknowledges as having influenced his views in this area: Spinoza. Then I'll ask whether or not it tallies with the other outlined properties of structuralism. In discussing each feature, I shall raise the question whether Althusser's picture can be applied to that of Marx. To anticipate a little, I believe that, in so far as Althusser is a structuralist, he is not a follower of Marx and vice versa.

Society or at least some abstraction from it is described by Althusser as a 'complex whole' which has '...the unity of a structure articulated in dominance.'[27] He contrasts this whole with the 'Hegelian' totality and the type of totality assumed by 'mechanistic materialists'.[28] He believes that these two mistaken positions derive from common presuppositions. What is common to the two viewpoints, and the respect in which they are both wrong, is their belief that one can 'read off' an understanding of the essence of some phenomenon by looking at its appearances. (This doctrine appears in 'empiricism', the view from which Althusser derives 'mechanical' materialism as 'abstractionism', and it appears in Hegel as the theory that the events in history are to be treated as manifestations of the Idea.)

Althusser claims that he and Hegel have in common the use of the word 'totality'[29] but that the conceptions to which the word refers in each case are vastly different. The Hegelian totality is 'simple';[30] every 'concrete difference' featured in (it) for example civil society the state, religion, philosophy etc. is 'negated as soon as (it is) affirmed'.[31]

In Hegel, according to Althusser, '(all the concrete differences are) no more than "moments" of the simple internal principle of the totality, which fulfils itself by negating the alienated difference that it posed; further as alienations – phenomena – of the simple internal principle, these differences are all equally '*indifferent*', that is practically equal beside it ... and therefore equal to one another...'[32]

(Althusser's italics) In Hegel's *Philosophy of Right*, to give an example, the State is dealt with only in so far as it pertains to the course of development of the Idea.[33]

In contrast with the Hegelian 'totality', it looks as though Althusser's 'whole' fits tenet one of structuralism. His totality, his abstract model of society, is a 'complex' one 'structured-in-dominance'. It contains four levels or elements, each of which is itself structured and is described by Althusser as a 'practice'. Practice in general he characterises as 'any process of *transformation* of a determinate given raw material into a determinate *product*, a transformation effected by a determinate human labour, using determinate means (of "production").'[34] (Althusser's italics) There are four types of practice going to make up the totality: economic practice, political, ideological and theoretical practice. Economic practice is the practice of producing use-values by the activity of men and women working with means of production in production relations.[35] Political practice is organised on the basis of historical materialism, and which transforms *its* raw material – social relations – into new ones.[36] Ideological practice transforms its object: people's consciousness. And theoretical practice takes two forms: on the one hand it is 'ideological' theoretical practice – the forms that go to make up the pre-history of a science and their philosophies; and on the other it is 'scientific theoretical practice'. The term 'social practice', then, covers all of these types. Althusser tells us that every 'simple category' for example labour or production presupposes the structured whole of society.[37]

I believe that Althusser is conflating two types of explanation here. He confuses a logical connection between two things with a factual – in this case historical – relation between them. He says that every 'simple category' presupposes the existence of the structured whole of society. One might interpret 'presuppose' here either in a logical or in a factual historical manner. Viewed in the former way, Althusser's view is structuralist and conforms with the thinking of his mentor, Spinoza. It is also compatible with his sympathetic reference to Marx's critique of the concept 'production-in-general'. However, Althusser's view, on this reading, does not allow us to make sense of other aspects of Marx's thought. Understood in the latter fashion, Althusser's picture makes sense of some examples of Marx and of the actual evidence he, Althusser, presents in favour of his picture. Seen like this, however, not only is Althusser not a structuralist by criterion one, but his thinking does not fit with the ideas of Spinoza. Moreover, his ideas are compatible with a rather boring reading of 'production-in-general' which is quite definitely out of tune with Marx's critique of the concept. So Althusser's structuralism conforms to one part of Marx's thinking but not to another; where he is not a structuralist, his thinking fails to fit a different Marx. In addition, his ideas do not then conform to those of his mentor Spinoza.

Althusser describes Spinoza as 'the only theoretician who had the unprecedented daring to pose (the problem of the determination of the elements of a whole by the structure of the whole) and outline a first solution to it ...'[38]

Let us look briefly at Spinoza in order to bring into the open the points of similarity between the two and to bring to light the conflict in Althusser's thinking.

In a letter, Spinoza paints a picture of a worm living inside the bloodstream. From the point of view of the worm, he suggests, each drop of blood appears to be independent and not part of a total system. But in fact, says Spinoza, the nature of each drop of blood and of the bloodstream itself can be understood only in the context of a larger system. The nature of the system of which the bloodstream is a part must be understood before one can identify each droplet of blood. Similarly, in any system, the system as a whole must be grasped before one can understand the part. The nature of the part is determined by its role in the whole system.[39]

The 'whole' in which Spinoza is interested is something he refers to as 'God or Nature' (or God and Nature; these being two names for the same thing).[40] The whole is a substance, which he defines as 'that which is in itself and is conceived through itself: in other words that the conception of which does not need the conception of another thing from which it must be formed.'[41] Substances 'have' attributes, which are defined as 'that which the intellect perceives of substance as constituting its essence.'[42] Attributes, D.F. Hallett says, do not 'inhere in a substance, rather they *constitute* its essence'.[43] Any proposition[44] attributing something to a substance will be exhibiting the essence of that substance. Since each proposition is doing this it will be a necessary truth. Spinoza does not accept the existence of contingent propositions. As Macyntre puts it: '(Spinoza) fail(s) to distinguish the identifying from the describing functions of expressions, he cannot distinguish between a substance incorrectly identified and a substance incorrectly described.'[45] All truths, for Spinoza, then, are necessary truths.

So, reverting to the example of the worm and the bloodstream, if the drop of blood is an attribute of the bloodstream in accordance with definition four (though this is open to question, since the blood-stream would not be a Spinozist 'substance' and even supposing it were, the drop of blood may not be one of its essential attributes) then the drop of blood 'presupposes' the bloodstream in a very special sense: any proposition asserting of the drop of blood that it is 'in' the bloodstream will be necessarily true, and the proposition 'that's a drop of blood' will be deductively related to the proposition: 'that's the bloodstream'.

Returning now to Althusser, if we interpret his claim to the effect that every 'simple category' presupposes the existence of the structured whole of society in Spinozist fashion, we have to say that every proposition expressing a relation between the social whole and one of its elements will be a necessary truth. But it is difficult to think of examples which make sense in this light. Some of Althusser's examples, following Marx, of simple categories are 'labour' and 'exchange'. Of the first, he says, 'the individual producer – the individual as the subject of production only appeared in developed capitalist society.' Here, individual economic activity presupposes the existence of capitalist society. And, of exchange, he says, quoting Marx, that it 'did not appear historically in all its intensity until the most developed states of society.'[46] He concludes, then, that 'it is the structured whole which gives its meaning to the simple category.'[47] Can one say that Althusser means to make out that all descriptions of exchange entail descriptions of society? This would be a highly implausible claim, and would not be what Marx intended.

Perhaps, rather than using quite this strong Spinozist sense of 'presuppose' Althusser means something weaker. According to P.F. Strawson: '... a statement S presupposes a statement S' in the sense that the truth of S' is a precondition of the truth or falsity of S... This is the relation between the statement that all John's children are asleep (S) and the statement that John has children, that there exist children of John's (S').[48] Similarly we could say 'an act of exchange has taken place' (S) and 'a society exists' (S'). As in the first case, the truth of S' is a precondition of the truth or falsity of S. But our second case is not so clear-cut as is that of Strawson. We can only get the appropriate relation if we build in the required assumption – namely that exchanges cannot take place outside of society. If society is defined in such a way as to make it true by definition that exchanges take place in it, the relation holds, but only in a trivial sense. So, if we interpret Althusser in Spinozist fashion, as he apparently wishes us to do, we cannot make much sense of the particular examples he offers us of 'simple categories' presupposing the existence of the structured whole. We could on a Spinozist reading of Althusser, however, make sense of Althusser's sympathetic reference to Marx's critique of 'production-in-general'. Production, on the Spinozist reading of Althusser, would be more like a large particular thing – more like Spinoza's God or Nature – than like a concept. It would not be something of which particular 'productions' were instances. Rather, particular acts of production would be simply exemplifications of 'production'. In producing a part of a car in the capitalist mode of production, I would be simply exemplifying production for exchange value.

So there is a way of making Althusser a structuralist by criterion one, but though this reading of him allows us to give a certain kind of meaning to one idea of Marx's, it does not make much sense of some of the examples from Marx Althusser himself cites.

These examples are made more intelligible if we interpret 'presuppose' in 'simple categories presuppose society' in an historical fashion. As a matter of historical fact, exchange and production did not appear outside of society; they presuppose society only in this weak sense. Althusser himself appears to read the examples this way. But, seen in this light, they do not of course justify any connection with Spinoza. Reading them this way, indeed, is compatible with referring to 'production-in-general' as Althusser sometimes seems to want to, as a general concept, which has instances. 'Production' in 'production presupposes society' is a particular case of the concept 'production-in-general'. It is conceivable (though unlikely) that there are other types of production occurring outside society.

So, the answer to the question: 'is Althusser a structuralist by criterion one?' can be either yes or no. If he is read à la Spinoza, he is a structuralist, but his own examples from Marx, then, make no sense. And if he is not read through the eyes of his mentor, he is not a structuralist. In such circumstances, however, Althusser fails to do justice to another theme of Marx.

What about the second criterion for being a structuralist? Althusser occasionally mentions the word 'system' and describes it as having a structure,[49] so at least sometimes he is a structuralist by this tenet. He does not discuss laws of coexistence (at least not by that name) instead he emphasises the particular type of causation 'metonymic causality' which is characteristic of his structuralism. What he actually means by 'cause' may be more like what others have characterised as 'coexistence'. So he may indeed be a structuralist by the third criterion. Let us have a look at Althusser's concept of causation in order to see whether he is a structuralist in the third sense.

Althusser and Causation

As with his picture of the nature of the totality, here too Althusser is influenced by Spinoza. In discussing the relationship of the structure to its elements, Althusser refers to the latter. He says: '... the structure is immanent in its effects, a cause immanent in its effects in the Spinozist sense of the term, that *the whole existence of the structure consists in its effects...*'[50] (Althusser's italics).

Let us look once more at Spinoza, this time to understand what he meant by cause. The cause of any being, for Spinoza, is that which makes it what it is. Causes produce their effects necessarily. 'From a given defined cause, an effect necessarily follows... If something is the adequate cause of something else, the latter can be adequately conceived through the former.'[51]

The conception of an effect depends upon and involves the conception of cause. 'X is not the cause of y' entails 'y cannot be understood by x'. There is thus a very close connection, for Spinoza, between the cause of a being (what makes it what it is) and the being's essential properties. To explain something causally is to show the necessary connection of the essential properties of a substance with the substance of which they are properties. That is to say, to explain something causally is to show, of an essential property, that that is what it is.

Spinoza's conception of causality is in marked contrast to that of the person whom many regard to be the prime representative of the empiricist tradition: David Hume. According to Hume, the connection between cause and effect is never necessary; it is always conceivable that a given cause might be conjoined with the negation of its usual effect.[52] Causal relations are analysed as regular succession of the effect upon the cause. Not only is the notion of necessary connection between cause and effect exhumed from Hume's analysis, but so too is any idea of causal power or agency.

In a sense, then, Spinoza's conception of causality is more like a law of coexistence than like a law of succession: if, for instance, a table is defined as a body with four legs and a top, then possessing four legs and a top is necessarily part of what makes the table what it is. The legs and the top 'coexist' in the table. But it would be harder to understand successive phenomena in this Spinozist light. So if Althusser's conception of cause fits that of his mentor Spinoza, as he wants it to, then he is a structuralist by criterion three.

Althusser makes much of what he describes as his 'Spinozist' conception of causality. 'The structure' he says, 'is not an essence *outside* the economic phenomena which comes to alter their aspect, forms and relations and which is effective on them as an absent cause, *absent because it is outside them. The absence of the cause in the structure's "metonymic causality" on its effects is not the fault of the exteriority of the structure with respect to the economic phenomena; on the contrary, it is the very form of the interiority of the structure, as a structure, in its effects.'*[53] (Althusser's italics)

One thing that emerges from this is that the 'essence' of a structure is not something 'underlying' its appearance, a 'transcendent' reality distinct from the knowable realm. (This appears to conflict with other readings of Althusser where he is an epistemological realist.) Rather, for Althusser here, the essence of a structure is nothing over and above its appearance. Essence and appearance coincide.[54] Of course, it is possible that there is no conflict with the other Althusser; essence and appearance may coincide, but the two may not be seen to coincide. Metaphysically, they may be identical, but because of human limitations, men and women may be unaware of their identity. Something like this was Locke's view of the relation between the real essence and the nominal essence of a substance. The real essence is the set of properties which causally account for the set of properties by means of which the substance is normally identified – the nominal essence. For example, the real essence properties of gold would include its atomic number, and some of its nominal essence properties would be its shiny yellow colour, its malleability etc. For most of us, though real essence is not known, it is not unknowable. But if we were God, real essence properties would become knowable and known and we would be able to see the necessary connection between real and nominal essence. In other words, real essence properties and those in the nominal essence would coincide.

Does this Lockean reading of the relation between reality and appearance fit Marx, whose views, in one guise, Althusser is presenting? Althusser mentions Marx's doctrine of fetishism as a phenomenon for which his picture is appropriate.[55] One case of that doctrine is the following: really wages are equivalent to the cost of reproducing the labourer (and sometimes, his family). Really the labourer works longer than is sufficient to produce an equivalent in value to the cost of reproducing him/herself. He or she produces surplus value for the capitalist. But it appears as though the labourer is being given an equivalent in value to that which he or she has contributed to producing. Is it appropriate to say that really essence and appearance coincide here, and it just seems to us that they differ? Of course, if we take appearance to be equivalent to what Marx described as reality, then the two will coincide. But Marx – and Althusser too – wants to make the point that the capitalist 'appearance' is as much 'reality' as is the one he has analysed. And surely it is just not true that were we God – were we to have perfect knowledge of existing reality, of capitalist social relations – essence and appearance would coincide. The distinction Marx drew attention to between the essence and appearance of the capitalist world would not disappear just through our coming to *understand* the reality – on the contrary, action has to be taken to do away with it. In this respect, the distinction between essence and appearance in Marx's analysis of capitalism is absolutely unlike that, for instance, in a Lockean substance. One could offer a parallel argument against the Spinozist reading of Althusser on cause and the relation between appearance and reality fitting this example from Marx. Marx would have disagreed just as much with the Spinozist claim that appearance and reality coincide, as he does with the Lockean view that really they coincide, but they are not seen to be the same by us limited beings.

And the emphasis on the appearance disappearing into the reality is very different from Althusser's Spinozist emphasis, which is on the 'structure' or the 'essence' being nothing outside its 'effects'; in other words, he seems to want to collapse the distinction in favour of the appearance. So it does not make much sense to describe the examples from Marx as cases where 'really' essence and 'appearance' coincide, only it seems otherwise to us, limited, human beings. It appears then that there is, indeed, a conflict between the 'realist' reading of Althusser and the Spinozist reading.

Where we take the 'Spinozist' reading of Althusser, then, it is plausible to say that he is a 'structuralist' by criterion three. But as in our discussion of the first property of 'structuralism' here too it appears that, to the extent that Althusser is a 'structuralist' he cannot claim to be analysing Marx.

Perhaps, however, we can get a 'structuralist' reading of Althusser, by this criterion, and one which is compatible with Marx, if we look elsewhere in Althusser for an understanding of the way in which he applies the concept of cause.

Cause: Another Attempt

Remember that, for Spinoza, causes and effects are necessarily related to one another. There is another important feature of cause, for him, which on the face of it appears to be in conflict with the necessary relationship between the two. This is that the concept of cause is 'conceived as action'.[56] How are these two ideas reconciled in Spinoza? The answer is that the concept of activity, here, is that of making explicit something which is already latently there: it is activity in the sense in which the proof of a theorem could be said to involve the activity of applying axioms and rules. The 'effect', the theorem, is produced from the 'cause': the axioms and rules. So, the cause 'contains' the effect.

It may be that this Spinozist concept of cause is relevant to Althusser's conception of reading, for Althusser says: '... a philosophical reading of *Capital* is only possible as the application of that which is the very object of our investigation, Marx's philosophy ... It is therefore a question of producing, in the precise sense of the word, which seems to signify making manifest what is latent.'[57]

This passage is directly reminiscent of Spinoza. In order to understand the way in which the concept of cause has application, we must examine the theory of reading. Let us look at this theory, and see whether we can produce an interpretation of Althusser's structuralism in this sense, which is compatible with Marx.

Reading

The notion of reading, for Althusser, is connected in some way with the question of the scientificity of what is expressed in *Capital*: 'We read *Capital* (in order to pose) the question of scientific discourse.'[58]

Reading should not be 'innocent'. '... there is no such thing as an innocent reading ...'[59] 'Innocent readings' go along with 'the empiricist conception of knowledge'.[60] Althusser dislikes the conception of knowledge which, in his view, underpins a technique, and not a particular technique or particular techniques of reading. (One could of course criticise a technique without criticising the view of knowledge underlying it – one might suggest that a technique of for instance placing emphasis upon particular words when reading Eliot's *The Waste Land* fails to do justice to the meaning of the poem.)

Althusser criticises 'innocent readings' for viewing the relation between the text and its subject matter as an 'expressive' one. This, as we already know, is an empiricist way of seeing the relation. As an example of an innocent reading, take our reading of Marx's *Capital*: 'When we read Marx, we immediately find a *reader* who *reads* to us, and out loud.'[61] (Althusser's italics) When Marx reads to us 'innocently', '(he) reads his predecessors discourse (Smith's for instance) through his own discourse'.[62] When he reads in this way, Marx's text is just Smith's with a few things added.

Althusser is concerned, not with methods of reading, generally, nor with just any method of reading *Capital*. He is interested quite specifically in the way to read *Capital* in order to understand Marx's relation to the classical political economists. The question of the scientificity of historical materialism is seen here as that of Marx's relation to Smith and Ricardo. So Althusser makes certain assumptions about the way of going about answering the question of scientificity.

On the face of things there are some similarities between Althusser's conception of reading and that of Derrida (although Derrida is, in fact, critical of earlier 'structuralisms'). According to the latter, the text is a 'de-centred structure'.[63] There is an infinite number of possible 'readings' of a text. Each act of consuming the text produces a different reading of it. The text is not a given entity with a fixed meaning. Rather a particular meaning is produced by a reading from the 'semiotic field'. The text is, as it were, 'produced' in the process of reading or consuming it.

The text, for Althusser too, is not simply given. Its meaning is produced by the reading of it. And where there are similarities there are shared difficulties. The text ceases to have any identity – how does one distinguish *King Lear* from *The Third Policeman?* The words on the page might produce identical 'readings' of each. But there are differences between Althusser and Derrida. There may be an infinity of possible readings of a text for Althusser, as for Derrida, but for him only one of these results in a knowledge. Only one reading of *Capital* is correct from the viewpoint of uncovering the scientificity of historical materialism.

We will see that Althusser's picture is directly reminiscent of Spinoza's view of the 'production' of nature by God: nature is a necessary effect of God's productivity, as the proof of a theorem is the necessary effect of the application of axioms and rules. In Althusser, the text and the theory of scientificity are the necessary effects of a reading of the text. In order to see how this is, we will need to take a little detour.

Lecture Symptomatique

Spinoza, according to Althusser, gives us the beginnings of a correct view of reading. Spinoza proposed: '... a philosophy of the opacity of the immediate.'[64] Spinoza 'linked together (in this way) the essence of reading and the essence of history in a theory of the difference between the imaginary and the true'.[65]

The correct view of reading is what Althusser calls 'symptomatic': 'lecture symptomatique'. On this conception, we must not understand Marx as having operated with the same assumptions as the classical political economists but simply to have seen more than they did, on those assumptions. We must not read the texts of Smith and Ricardo as containing gaps which Marx filled in. On the contrary: '... what classical political economy does not see, is not what it does not see, it is *what it sees*; it is not what it lacks, on the contrary, it is what it does not lack; it is not what it misses, on the contrary, it is *what it does not miss*.'[66] (Althusser's italics) 'The oversight, then, is not to see what one sees, the oversight no longer concerns the object, but *the sight* itself.'[67] (Althusser's italics) So what is wrong with the classical political economists is contained in their texts: what they see, conceals what they don't see; and in order to see what they don't see, what they do see had to be eliminated from the field of vision or at least radically transformed.

Considering the texts of Smith, Ricardo and Marx, the theory Althusser comes up with is as follows; he quotes from Marx's *Capital*, Chapter XIX, on wages.[68] Marx, in that passage, is dealing with the classical political economists' calculations of the value of labour. Marx tells us that the classical political economists began by asking how the price of labour is determined. They recognised that oscillations in supply and demand could explain not the price of labour, but only the variation in price around a certain norm. As soon as supply and demand balanced, the price of labour no longer depended on their action, and must be determined by something else. He argues that, in their view, the necessary price or Adam Smith's 'natural price' or the value of labour, is determined by the value of subsistence goods necessary for the maintenance and reproduction of the labourer. Althusser, quoting Marx, goes on: '*It thus unwittingly changed terrain* by substituting for the value of labour, up to this point, *the apparent object of its investigations* the value of labour power, a power which only exists in the personality of the labourer, and is as different from its function, labour, as a machine is from its performance.'[69] (Althusser's italics) And he continues: 'The result the analysis led to, therefore, was *not a resolution of the problem.*[70] (Althusser's italics) Althusser says of this that the classical political economists produced a correct answer to a question that was never posed. He mentions Engels' *Preface* to Vol. 2 *of Capital*, where Engels compares the relation of Marx to the classical political economists to that between Lavoisier and Priestley.

Just as Priestley, and phlogistic chemistry, produced oxygen, so the classical political economists *produced* surplus value. It was left to Lavoisier, however, to *identify* the substance Priestley produced. And it was left to Marx to *identify* surplus value. Althusser suggests that the texts of Smith and Ricardo are at fault. He formulates the appropriate sentence of the classical political economists in two possible ways as follows.

(i) '*The value of labour* [...] *is equal to the value of the subsistence goods necessary for the maintenance and reproduction of labour.*'[71] (Althusser's italics).

and

(ii) *The value of labour is equal to the value of the subsistence goods necessary for the maintenance and reproduction of the labourer.*[72] (Althusser's italics)

And he says: '(the first) sentence means nothing: what is the maintenance of "labour?" what is the reproduction of "labour?"'[73] And in the second sentence, 'the term at the end of the sentence (now) clashes with the term at the beginning: they do not have the same content and the equation cannot be made, for it is not the labourer who is bought for wages, but his "labour".'[74] Althusser goes on to tell us that there is present in the answer the absence of its question. Marx can go on, he tells us, to 'pose the unuttered *question*', simply by 'uttering the concept present in an unuttered form in the emptiness in the *answer*.'[75] (Althusser's italics)

How does the theory look? The examination of the text of *Capital* is to play a crucial role in determining historical materialism's scientificity. How exactly does it do this? We will find the answer by examining another concept which is important as far as the scientificity of historical materialism is concerned. Marx, in *Capital*, produced a new object: labour power. Implied in the production of this new object was 'a transformation of the *entire* terrain and its *entire* horizon, which are the background against which the new problem is produced ... the production of a new problem endowed with this *critical* character (critical in the sense of a critical situation) is the unstable index of the production of a new theoretical *problematic*, of which this problem is only one symptomatic mode.'[76] (Althusser's italics)

Problematic

Can the concept 'problematic' throw light on the technique of reading *Capital* and its relevance for the theory of scientificity and can it reveal a sense of Althusser's structuralism which is compatible with Marx? To facilitate answering these questions, it would be useful to list a few occurrences of the concept, in Althusser himself, and in a couple of his commentators. A. Callinicos says:

'... the concept of theory's problematic becomes that of the underlying structure which renders possible the raising of certain questions in a particular form, while ruling out the raising of others.'[77]

And Callinicos compares Althusser's concept with Lakatos' heuristic: 'the theoretical structures that made (scientific) discoveries possible'.[78]

There is one usage in Althusser which accords more or less with this. In discussing the young Marx, Althusser says: '... it is not so much the immediate content of the objects reflected as the way the problems are posed which constitutes the ultimate ideological essence of an ideology.'[79]

So, in this sense, problematic has to do with the presuppositions of a theory, and not with the concept of reading a text.

Ben Brewster, in his Glossary to *For Marx*, characterises 'problematic' as the view that: 'A word or a concept cannot be considered in isolation; it only exists in the theoretical or ideological framework in which it is used, its problematic ... It should be stressed that problematic is not a world view. It is not the essence of the thought of an individual or epoch which can be deduced from a body of texts by an empirical, generalizing reading; it is centred on the *absence* of problems and concepts within the problematic as much as their presence, it can therefore only be realised by a symtomatic reading (lecture symptomale q.v.) on the model of the Freudian analyst's reading of his patients utterances.'[80]

Brewster mentions the notion of reading in his account of 'Problematic'. A problematic, he says is *realised* by a symptomatic reading. And he compares the latter notion with Freud's procedure.

So there are at least two senses of 'problematic' in operation in Althusser. Paul Patton distinguishes two senses of the term, a pair of senses which corresponds to those I have distinguished. On the one hand, problematic ... may refer to the conditions of historical existence of a science, which are external to it ... On the other hand, problematic refers, in the case of a science, to the "conditions" which define the science as such, that is, which define the formal and semantic rules the observation of which is required in order that a statement belong to the science, and which governs the intelligibility of its discourse. These conditions are internal to the discourse of the science itself.'[81]

Patton goes on to illustrate the distinction by pointing out that as far as the latter sense of 'problematic' goes, Marx's conception of the capitalist mode of production and exchange implies a non-Hegelian theory of the form of the social totality and its parts; whereas, as far as the first sense goes, 'Hegel's conception represents an essential, historical condition of the possibility of Marx's critique of political economy.'[82]

It is the second, Spinozist sense of 'problematic' which is relevant to the outlined picture of reading. Althusser is drawing both on Freud and on Spinoza.

Let us take Freud's *Interpretation of Dreams* procedure for illumination. In interpreting a dream Freud pays as much attention to the 'errors' and 'omissions' of the dream as he does to what he terms its 'manifest' content.[83]

The latter, in his terminology, is a 'condensed' and 'displaced' version of the dream thoughts.[84] It is by enlarging on the manifest dream content and replacing some of it that one arrives at the latent *dream thoughts*. The latter are responsible for the dream; and the dream has the *function* of fulfilling wishes which are expressed in those thoughts.

Freud 'reads' a dream in a particular way, taking into account 'absences' in it, which he obtains from elsewhere, in order to arrive at the latent dream thoughts. Althusser reads a text in a particular way, also taking into account 'absences' which he, too, gets from elsewhere, in order to obtain the problematic of that text. And sometimes that problematic will contain the theory of scientificity (for the science expressed in that text). In Althusser's view, just as Marx 'symptomatically reads' the classical political economists, so do we 'symptomatically read' Marx's *Capital*. We read it in this way in order to uncover Marx's philosophy – or the theory of scientificity for *Capital*. In fact Marx employed philosophical concepts which were 'essential to his thought, but absent from his discourse'.[85] And, just as the classical political economists produced an answer to a question they were unable to pose, so did Marx produce the answer to a question he did not 'have time' to pose; the question, namely '... what is the specific difference distinguishing the Marxist dialectic from the

Hegelian dialectic?'[86] Althusser 'reads' *Capital* from a particular point of view, taking into account what is not there as much as what is there, and obtains, by this means, the theory of scientificity, or Marx's philosophy. Althusser reads *Capital* in this way and causally 'produces', in Spinozist fashion, the theory of scientificity. Just as the proof of a theorem is 'contained in' the axioms and rules, and its production is the production of what is already, latently, there; so too the production of the theory of scientificity is an act of making manifest what is already, latently, there. The theory of reading is crucially required for uncovering Marx's philosophy. The Spinozist conception of the causal relation between 'appearance' and reality has a clear application: the 'problematic', the appearance, is the set of techniques employed to uncover the 'reality': the theory of scientificity in *Capital*.

But there are difficulties with this Spinozist/Freudian picture. Indeed the Freudian influence clashes with the Spinozist one to produce a problem for Althusser. Which absences need to be taken into account in the reading of *Capital*? Clearly it is not just any old idea which happens not to be in the text – the theme of Blake's *Marriage of Heaven and Hell* for instance. In Freud's case, we know the answer: the *relevant* absences are culled from the waking thoughts of the individual whose dream is undergoing analysis. (And it may be a problem for Freud whether or not the decision as to which thoughts are to be considered the appropriate ones makes the whole procedure of analysis circular.) But what are the relevant absences in Althusser? If we assume that what he says he takes into account gives us some idea of what he considers to be relevant, he tells us that the absences *contain* Marx's philosophy. And here we get the Spinozism.

A philosophical reading of *Capital* constitutes the causal 'production' in the Spinozist sense, of what is already there. An uncharitable interpretation of Althusser here would be to say that he is simply 'reading in' to Marx's text what he wants to find. Marx himself could not have produced the rules and procedure necessary to understand the scientificity of his own theory, for 'the age Marx lived in did not provide him, and he could not acquire in his lifetime, an adequate concept with which to think what he produced: the concept of the effectivity of a structure on its elements.'[87] We could say, then, that Althusser is 'reading in' to his understanding of Marx's text the very generalisation he wants to discover. Might there not be other techniques which are 'latent' in Marx's text? How do we know that Althusser's is the right one? Why should we accept his reading?

There seems to be a crucial disanalogy between the type of case Spinoza offered us and the one Althusser is presenting us with. It makes sense to say that the axioms and rules are 'latent' in the proof of a theorem and that if the proof works out, the axioms and theorems were the right ones. And similarly, because of the properties God is supposed to possess, according to Spinoza, it makes sense to talk of God being latent in nature and God as cause with Nature as effect being the 'right' cause. But it doesn't make sense in the same way to refer to Althusser's problematic being the 'right' one for the production of the theory of scientificity in *Capital*, because it does not make sense to refer to the relation between the problematic and the theoretical object as a necessary one in the way that the others are. So there could be other possible 'problematics' and it becomes viciously circular of Althusser to 'read in' to his understanding of particular sciences the very generalisation he wants to discover.

It seems, then, that if Althusser's Spinozist notion of cause is like the structuralist 'law of coexistence' then he is indeed a structuralist by criterion three. This time his structuralism has led him into a different kind of difficulty. Whereas, in the previous two cases, Althusser's views either fitted the tenets of 'structuralism' but did not tally with the ideas of Marx or complied with the ideas of Marx but not of structuralism; this time the problem is different. Althusser is trying to answer a question he thinks is latent in Marx, the question namely; 'Is historical materialism scientific?' And this time his structuralism prevents him from answering that question in a non-circular fashion.

Althusser is at pains to emphasise that the 'social formation' is not revealed for what it is to the untutored eye: grasping it requires that one penetrate the appearances. So he is a structuralist by the fifth criterion. Here indeed, he is like Marx; in several places Marx holds a similar view.

If one takes 'structuralism' to indicate a trend, it is not necessary that every structuralist exhibit all of the features picked out as characteristic of the trend, nor indeed that any individual should uphold all of the features. Such tidy fitting of the facts is not characteristic of for example the 'Enlightenment' or Protestantism any more than it need be of structuralism. Althusser is a structuralist in so far as his thought fits at least some of the properties of the phenomenon. So, although A. Schaff may be right when he criticises Althusser for using terms ambiguously and for lacking in logical precision,[88] he is going too far when he refers to Althusser's thought as 'pseudo-structuralism'.[89] Timpanaro, too, is too critical when he labels 'French structuralism' (including Althusser's) as 'sophisticated charlatanry'; and talks about 'old literary foxes who, as their final and most sophisticated trick, have taken to 'playing at science'.[90]   If fitting the principles of structuralism makes one a structuralist, then Althusser is one, and not a 'pseudo' one.

Conclusion

It seems that there is some evidence that Althusser fits the structuralist bill, though it is difficult to give any overall conception of the nature of his version of the view. Sometimes his thinking is ambiguous and only one of the interpretations of his thinking is a 'structuralist' one. Clearly he believes in 'wholes' and he believes in them as something more than the sum of their elements. Furthermore the conception of cause with which he is sympathetic makes his view out to be closer to the structuralist one of emphasising laws of coexistence rather than causal laws in the sense of relations between temporally distinct items. Despite his renunciation of the structuralist label his thinking is close to structuralism in several ways. But, often where Althusser is a structuralist, he cannot be described as a Marxist. His structuralism is frequently in conflict with the ideas of Marx. In the next chapter, I shall discuss Marx's work in more detail.

2
Economism

Althusser proposed his 'structuralist' reading of Marx partly as an alternative to 'economism'.[1] Largely following him, 'economistic' versions of Marxism have come under severe attack recently; indeed it is sometimes taken for granted that 'economistic' Marxism is wrong. Because of this assumption, I believe that the issue is worth attending to in its own right, as it appears not just in Althusser. Althusser did not coin the term economism; it occurs in Lenin, for instance, but he employed it extensively, and contemporary usage of the word is coloured by his thinking. As we shall see, although recent understanding of the meaning of the term comes largely from Althusser, there is in fact considerable variation in the actual sense it is given by different people. Because of this diversity of interpretation, attacking someone for holding an 'economistic' position can turn out to be very unspecific. Furthermore, I believe that on at least some definitions of 'economism', Marx is an economistic thinker; and I would like to show how this is. If one criticises Marxists for holding an economistic variation of Marxism, one must criticise Marx himself too.

Following upon the publication of G.A. Cohen's seminal treatise, *Marx's Theory of History, A Defence*[2], this is no longer a controversial thing to say. I would like, however, to rehearse some of the arguments again, particularly in relation to Althusser's thought.

Following Cohen and others, it might be accepted that Marx is an 'economistic' thinker (although Althusser himself would not hold this view) and it might be argued that Althusser's theory – understood now as a position standing on its own feet as a rewritten version of Marx – is superior to that of Marx. One reason why it might be held to be superior is that it allows us to explain 'the oppression of women' as distinct from class exploitation. Ted Benton, for one, gives as one reason for the inadequacy of classical Marxism on the question of gender, its 'economic reduction--ism'.[3] Marx's materialism, it could be said, does not allow us to give a non-reductionist account of women's oppression. So I shall go on to argue, in subsequent chapters, that one can accommo-

24

date an analysis of 'the oppression of women' within Marx's perspective.

Althusser and Balibar

Althusser characterises 'economism' so: 'According to the economistic or mechanistic hypothesis, the role of the essence/phenomena opposition is to explain the non-economic as a phenomenon of the economic, which is its essence.'[4] Balibar, in *Reading Capital*, characterises 'economism' as: '(a theory) which claims precisely to reduce all the non-economic instances of the social structure purely and simply to reflections, transpositions of phenomena of the economic base.'[5]

Althusser and Balibar identify economism as a view according to which non-economic phenomena are 'reduced to' economic ones. Presumably what they mean is, for instance, that something ideological – for example the Protestant ethic – would be redescribed in economic, perhaps in class terms. Protestantism would be simply an aspect of class exploitation: it would not have a separate existence. The non-economic and the economic would become one and the same. They identify 'economism' with the politics of the Second International. They further make out that the humanist and historicist ways of thinking which they characterise as a 'vital reaction against the mechanism and economism of the Second International'[6] have nevertheless 'rediscovered the basic theoretical principles of the Second International's economistic and mechanistic interpretation.'[7] They say that: 'there are really two distinct ways of identifying the superstructure with the infrastructure, or consciousness with the economy – one which sees in consciousness and politics only the economy, while the other imbues the economy with politics and consciousness, there is never more than one *structure* of identification at work – the structure of the problematic which, by reducing one to the other, *theoretically* identifies the two levels present.'[8] (Althusser's italics)

First I shall discuss Althusser's theory as a response to economism. In my view, on one reading of it, Althusser and Balibar fail to extricate themselves from economism; while on another reading of their theory, it is far removed from Marx's materialist conception of history.

I shall point to some of the senses the term 'economism' has acquired amongst writers subsequent to Althusser. The term is extensively used and it seems to be assumed that it has a clear meaning. In fact, however, 'economism' is used to mean a number of different things. Following that I will describe Marx's theory of the relation between 'base' and 'superstructure' and between 'conscious existence' and 'consciousness'. In the course of doing this, I shall argue that Marx is an economistic thinker by at least some definitions of the term.

Since Althusser and Balibar are critical of economistic thinkers for reducing the non-economic to the economic, we might expect from them an alternative account of the relation between the two. And it sometimes appears that this is what we are offered. Althusser quotes Marx:

> In all forms of society, it is a determinate production and its relations which assign every other production and its relations their rank and influence.'[9]

He goes on to explain that Marx is here discussing the 'determination of certain structures of production which are subordinate to a dominant structure of production, that is the determination of one structure by another and of the elements of a subordinate structure by the dominant, and therefore determinant structure.'[10]

The various 'structures' referred to here are the different practices going to make up the social formation.

What Althusser is describing here is the relation between the various levels in the structure. How are we to understand these relations? The answer, surely, is by referring to the Spinozist conception of causality. Economic and non-economic practices will be related, not by means of Humean or Leibnizean causality, but by Spinozist 'metonymic' causality. Now if we are to suppose that economic and non-economic phenomena are causally related, but causally related à la Spinoza; then the type of relation involved will be logical necessity. An economic description, for example 'that factory worker is exploited' will be deductively related to something non-economic, for example 'that factory worker is suffering from false consciousness.' False consciousness would have to be defined in terms of class exploitation in order that the appropriate deductive relation hold. And this, of course, is a form of reductionism. So, on this reading of Althusser, he does not escape economism as he himself characterises it.

But the above reading of Althusser may be somewhat unfair. The type of causation with which, it seems, he is really concerned, is not at all one which pertains to the relations between the elements in the social formation, but rather one which holds between the social formation as a whole and its elements. Spinoza, we remember him telling us, was the 'only theoretician who had the unprecedented daring' to pose the problem of 'the determination of the elements of the whole by the structure of the whole.'[11] So it seems that Althusser on one reading does not offer an account *at all* of the way in which the economic base of society relates to the elements of the superstructure. He is concerned, instead, with the relation between the whole and each of its elements. Not only are politics and ideology seen as 'effects' of something else, but so is the economy. Each of them is seen as an 'effect' of the structured whole.

This model, it seems to me, may bear some resemblance to Spinoza's thinking, but it has very little to do with Marx. Not only did Marx *not* make out that the 'social formation' as a whole has 'effects' in the Spinozist sense, but he *did* offer something of an account of the relations between the various levels in the social formation.

Economism

Here are some of the senses the term 'economism' has taken on. Some agree with Althusser about it. Thus Graham Locke tells us: 'To "forget about" the role of the superstructure in the reproduction of production relations; to want to explain everything (for example crises in capitalism or the transition to communism) by reference to the economic infrastructure alone, is of course *economism*.'[12] (Locke's italics)

In *Theoretical Practice*, we read that '(essentialism) includes reductionism, sociologism, geneticism etc. This general error sees every worker as essentially proletarian politically ... The reduction of levels of political position to class situation, or the conflation of levels, produces effects in the political position. From this vulgar Marxism, a crude economic determinism springs ultra-leftist or rightist political positions, rigidity in organisation, and ferocious sectarianism, since the essentialist element (the workers, the blacks etc.) are the source of the true line.'[13] Economism here is equated with a number of other 'errors', including economic determinism.

Poulantzas is critical of the economist reading of class, according to which: 'social class is located only at the level of the *relations of production* conceived in an economist fashion i.e. reduced to the position of agents in the labour process and to the means of production.'[14]

Classes, he says, are never simply related to the relations of production. According to him the concept class refers to the *'ensemble of the structures* of a mode of production and social formation *and to the relations which are maintained there* by the different levels.'[15] (Poulantzas' italics) So, according to Poulantzas, economistic readings of class 'reduce it' to the relations of production.

Richard Johnson characterises 'economism' as a 'mechanical determinism' and describes Maurice Dobb's history as 'the limit case of economism'.[16] Banaji refers to Dobb as an 'economistic' historian, and suggests that, for him, 'modes of production were deducible, by a relation of "virtual identity", from the given forms of exploitation of labour.'[17] In vulgar 'economistic' conceptions, a wage labourer is one who is forced to sell his labour-power. Labour power is a simple category. A consequence of Dobb's view, he argues, is that we would be forced to say that when thirteenth century English feudal estates were based almost entirely on wage labour, they were capitalist.

Economism, then, has taken on a number of different meanings. We will see that Marx was indeed someone who fell foul of the label in at least some of its senses. In order to show this let us look at Marx's picture of the relation between 'base' and 'superstructure'. I believe that Marx's theory of history is what some people have described as a 'technological determinism'. Crudely, I take this to be the view that human history is to be explained by the development of the productive forces. (Shaw and Cohen describe Marx's theory as a 'technological' theory).[18] According to technological determinism, alterations in the 'forces' of production are causally responsible for changes in the relations of production; and similarly a variation in the relations causally brings about a difference in the superstructure.

Marx on Forces and the Base

It is generally agreed that the 1859 *Preface*[19] to the *Contribution to the Critique of Political Economy* offers the most conclusive support for the technological determinist or 'economistic' interpretation of Marx's theory of history. In that work, the relations of production are said to constitute the 'economic structure of society'; these 'condition' the superstructure and corresponding forms of social consciousness, and they are transformed when they impede, rather than facilitate, the growth of the productive forces. This 'fettering' initiates an 'era of social revolution' which ends when 'new, higher relations of production' come into being. The production forces expand and develop in history.

The 1859 *Preface* is the text on which several protagonists of the 'economistic' reading of Marx's theory have relied. Plekhanov, for example, describes the *Preface* as 'a genuine "algebra" – and purely materialist at that – of social development'.[20] Plekhanov was a Menshevik and a critic of the Russian Revolution as premature, on historical materialist principles. But the Bolshevik sympathiser Bukharin, too, deems Marx's theory a technological determinism on the authority of the 1859 *Preface*. More recently, both G.A. Cohen and his student, H. Shaw, whose book *Marx's Theory of History* appeared almost contemporaneously with that of Cohen, rely heavily for their technological determinist reading of Marx on the *Preface*.

It is worth pointing out that the *Preface*, written in 1859, lies well within the purview of Marx's 'mature' period, on Althusser's division of his work into the pre-scientific, 'ideological' early Marx, and the 'scientific' late Marx. It is therefore stronger evidence against Althusser's claim that the 'real' Marx is not economistic than would be quotation from an early text. However, although out of context quotation is weak evidence, it is worth pointing to passages from Marx's early writings which offer some slender support to the view that Marx was an economistic thinker *throughout* his lifetime. For example:

From the *Poverty of Philosophy*: 'the relations correspond to a definite development of men and their productive forces and a change in men's productive forces necessarily brings about a change in their relations of production.'[21] From *Marx to Annekov*: '... as men develop their productive forces, that is, as they live, they develop certain relations with one another and that the nature of these relations is bound to change with the change and growth of these productive forces.'[22]

From the *German Ideology*: 'In the place of an earlier form of intercourse, which has become a fetter, a new one is put, corresponding to the more developed productive forces.'[23]

I could spend an inordinate amount of space (as, for example, Norman Geras has done with his 'reading' of the 6th Thesis on Feuerbach)[24] offering different possible interpretations of these passages. I shall say only that the passages quite clearly state that the forces of production are separate from the relations (contrary to

Balibar in *Reading Capital* pp. 233–5, 247) and that a change in the former 'necessarily brings about' an alteration in the latter. Whatever that expression does mean, the direction of alteration is quite plainly articulated.

The *Communist Manifesto* speaks, as does the 1859 *Preface*, of the feudal relations of production becoming 'fetters' on the 'already developed' productive forces.

From the 1848 *Communist Manifesto*:

the feudal organisation of agriculture and manufacturing industry, in one word, the feudal relations of property become no longer compatible with the already developed productive forces; they become so many fetters.[25]

Finally, I shall mention two further quotations: one from *Grundrisse*, which, as Gregory Elliott points out, although it comes within the ambit of Marx's mature works, Althusser scarcely acknowledges; and the other from *Theories of Surplus Value*. Both fit the general pattern of the other quotations.

Thus the social relations within which individuals produce, the social relations of production, change, are transformed, with the change and development of the material means of production, the productive forces.[26]

In the last analysis, their community, as well as the property based on it, reduces itself into a specific stage in the development of the productive forces of working subjects.[27]

Before going on to analyse in a little more detail the nature of the connection between forces and relations of production, I shall describe them. I propose to begin with the forces.

The Forces

Forces of production include at least instruments of production and raw materials on the one hand, and human labour power on the other. The clearest formulation of their nature is given by Cohen. He characterises a productive force so: '(to count as a productive force, a facility must be) capable of use by a producing agent in such a way that production occurs (partly) as a result of its use, and it is someone's

purpose that the facility so contribute to production. But that someone need not be the immediate producer himself. He could be a non-
producer in charge of the process.'[28] Cohen wishes to distinguish
productive forces from 'other requisites to and stimuli to production'.[29] He wants to exclude a soldier from being productive when he
supplies security essential to uninterrupted agrarian labour.[30] The
soldier's activity, he says, 'enables production but he is not productive ... Only what contributes materially within and to productive
activity as Marx demarcates it counts as a productive force.'[31]

This latter formulation of Cohen's seems to conflict with the earlier definition and there are counter-examples to his original definition. A car worker does not make a product; he or she contributes to
making it. And the railway worker expends labour power but does
not either make or contribute to making a product. It seems that it is
misleading too for Cohen to invoke Marx's distinction between labour which is productive and labour which is not in the discussion
of what is a productive force. Marx calls productive labour either
labour which is productive in general, that is useful labour, or which
is productive under capitalism. Useful labour is the production of
use-values through the labour process.[32] Productive labour under
capitalism is that which creates surplus value: 'The only worker
who is productive is one who produces surplus value for the capitalist, or in other words contributes towards the self valorisation of
capital ...'[33] And *only labour which is directly transformed into capital is
productive.'*[34] (Marx's italics)

Productive labour under capitalism, then, is labour exchanged
with capital to produce surplus value. Such labour is contrasted
with labour which is unproductive; namely labour which is exchanged with revenue.

Many groups of workers – teachers, nurses, air traffic controllers
– may not be productive in either of Marx's senses, and yet they
expend labour power in labouring activity. It could be argued that
they neither produce use-values nor create surplus value yet they
might count as being productive in the sense of contributing materially within and to productive activity.

Marx also sometimes demarcates the 'mode of co-operation of
workers' a productive force: 'By social we understand the co-operation of several individuals, no matter under what conditions, in
what way, and to what end. It follows from this that a certain mode
of production, or industrial stage, is always combined with a certain
mode of co-operation or social stage, and this mode of co-operation
is itself a "productive force".[35] Miller refers to other passages from

the *Grundrisse*, where modes of co-operation are designated productive forces.[36]

Cohen would deny that the mode of co-operation counts as a productive force, on the ground that it is a social property of society, while productive forces are material. However, I suggest that Marx's description of the mode of co-operation as social is misleading, and that one can describe it in such a way that it is material. Assuming, with Cohen, that productive forces are material it can therefore be a candidate for being a force.

Cohen offers the following criterion of the social: 'a description is social if and only if it entails an ascription to persons – specified or unspecified – of rights or powers vis a vis other men.'[37] An account of the mode of co-operation can be given which makes it non-social by this criterion. In every labour process (where more than one person works) there is a division of labour. In primitive communism tasks were divided amongst the population, although no-one enjoyed rights or powers over anyone else. And in the modern factory there is a division of tasks: people operate different parts of the assembly line. This is a division of tasks that can be described independently of the particular authority structure obtaining. Admittedly it may sometimes be true that the reason why a particular division of tasks is operative has to do with the authority structure; but this does not prevent one from describing the division of tasks independently of the system of rights or powers. One could, therefore, characterise the mode of co-operation, where it refers to the work relations that obtain independently of the authority structure, as 'material'. It is not material in quite the sense that Cohen would have it, it is not 'the process of production in general, occurring in all states of society ...'[38] for the division of labour takes different forms depending upon the society being described. Nonetheless the mode of co- operation is part of a description of the process whereby material goods are created, a description which does not entail the existence of rights or powers over people or things. (So, although Miller – see below – is not quite right to say that the mode of co-operation is included in 'what Cohen calls the material mode of production'[39] it is not part of the 'social' mode.)

I suggest, therefore, that productive forces could be characterised as follows: they are either used by an agent or agents who have divided their tasks to contribute to making a product or they are used in the servicing or transporting of such products. This amended definition still leaves out those things which I would agree with Cohen should be left out; namely laws, morals and government.

There is one other feature of productive forces Cohen alludes to which is worth mentioning. He says that 'x is a productive force only if ownership (or non-ownership) of x contributes to defining the position in the economic structure occupied by x's owner.'[40] But ownership of x in this sense is not sufficient for something being a productive force. The capitalists ownership of capital contributes to defining the position of the capitalist in the economic structure. But capital is not a productive force on either of the above characterisations of it.

Relations and Superstructure

I have now described productive forces. I said earlier that alterations in productive forces bring about a variation in the relations. What are the relations? Here I follow Cohen to the letter. Using the 1859 *Preface*, he describes the economic structure as being composed of productive relations and nothing but these.[41] The terms of production relations he gives as either persons or productive forces (in the sense of the restricted list: means of production and labour power); and the relations he describes as being 'either relations of ownership by persons of productive forces or persons or relations presupposing such relations of ownership... By ownership is here meant not a legal relationship but one of effective control.'[42] (Cohen's italics) (See Cohen Ibid. pp. 63–70 for a more detailed account of the notion of ownership and for a discussion of possible ownership positions of producers.)

As well as holding that alterations in the forces are responsible for bringing about a change in the relations, Marx makes out that a variation in the relations is causally responsible for a change in the superstructure. And, in addition, but separately, he proposes a more general view: that people's 'consciousness' is influenced by their 'social being'. I suggest that Marx uses the term 'superstructure' to refer to a fairly limited set of phenomena: as Cohen points out, according to Marx in the *Preface*, the superstructure is composed of political and legal institutions. Cohen takes the superstructure to be 'a set of non-economic institutions, notably the legal system and the state'. (For a more detailed discussion of the nature of the superstructure, including a problem raised by Acton, see Cohen chapter 8.)[43]

One might argue in favour of the technological determinist thesis by considering the alternatives to it, within the broad purview of

Marx's materialist conception of history. Using the letter (F) for the forces, (R) for the relations, (SS) for the superstructure, → to stand for a causal relation, and ↔ a two-way causal relation, these alternatives are as follows:

(1) (F) → (R) → (SS) or (F) → $\left(\begin{matrix} SS \\ R \end{matrix}\right)$

(2) (SS) ↔ (R)

(3) (R) are self-developing

(4) (F) ↔ (R)

There is also Althusser's own position, which has the forces 'determinant-in-the-last instance', but the relations, in certain circumstances, *dominant*.

(1) is the position I am defending. I will expand on what it means below. (2) is allowed by Marx in certain circumstances, as when, for example, he describes, in *Capital*, the altering pattern of capitalist control over the labour process, and the class struggle resulting from it. (This kind of enquiry has been continued by the CSE Labour Process group). But to attribute major alterations in the relations to superstructural change – to religion or legal matters, for example – runs directly contrary to Marx's materialism and could not be described as 'broadly within his perspective'.

As for (3): if there were no external impetus on the development of the relations, why should they change at all? Stagnation at a particular level would surely be an equally plausible option. Why, if the relations altered of their own accord, should certain types of conflict be insoluble in the existing social structure, as Marx argued is the case?

(4) is the position adopted by Mao, in his stricture to 'make the revolution and promote production'. But, like (3), it runs directly contrary to the quoted passages from Marx. Furthermore, if it were the correct interpretation of Marx, the claim that his theory of history is a *materialist* one would be difficult to sustain. Marx's claim, as I read it, is to the effect that historical change occurs, at bottom, because of *material* change. (It is not an ontological or an epistemological realism; rather it is, as Marx says it is, an *historical* materialism). (See my article.)[44]

If (4) was the correct reading of Marx, then he would, in effect, be saying that either material factors or non-material ones – relations between people for example – can bring about fundamental historical change. But this is emphatically *not* what he does say.

What does thesis (1), productive force determinism, actually mean? G.A. Cohen, as is well known, defends a functionalist interpretation of the thesis. His view, to do little justice to a complex thesis, is that the relations change because they are functional for the further development of the forces. I do not propose, in the limited space I have available, to argue against this thesis. Nor do I wish to spend time arguing for an alternative claim which may or may not be compatible with the functionalist perspective. I shall say only that, in my view, the quoted passages imply a causal thesis – namely that alterations in the forces are necessary and sufficient in certain circumstances for change to the relations. Marx does allow that superstructural phenomena may bring about an alteration in the relations – changes in the workplace may occur as a result of legal enactments, for example. Additionally, he would certainly argue that some force change may be accommodated within existing relations – an alteration to a machine in an assembly line, for example. But I would argue that these facts do not detract from the thesis that force change is necessary and sufficient for alteration in the relations.

Let us take two examples of superstructural change apparently bringing about an alteration in the relations: the 1842 Mines Act, which excluded women and children from underground work in the mines; and the 1844 Factory Act, which set a maximum twelve hour day for women factory workers, to exemplify this point. In fact, this legislation, rather than being generally benevolent towards the working classes, restricted the supply of what was seen as the least productive labour. (Feminists at the time indeed objected to this characterisation of women's capacities: women chainmakers in the period protested that they were as able as men were to wield heavy hammers. But the fact is that when women's labour has been necessary to maintain a certain level of development of the forces of production – as during wartime, for example – then legislation of the above sort is notable by its absence.) It came about when it did because of developments in machinery etc. Ultimately, the changes occurred then because of alteration in the forces.

As for cases where an alteration in the forces appears to be accommodated within the existing relations, here Marx's claim, I believe, would be that eventually the relations must change. Maybe they do not alter immediately, but they will in the long run.

The nature of the connection between forces and relations, I am suggesting, is causal – of the necessary and sufficient condition type.

Much more than this, of course, needs to be said about the precise character of the laws connecting particular sets of forces with particular sets of relations. I have said enough, however, for it to be clear that these causal laws are not deductive Spinozistic ones, as Althusser would have it. They may be either, broadly, 'realist' or Humean laws.

Force change, I am arguing, is necessary and sufficient, *in certain circumstances*, for an alteration in the relations. In fact, in the case of the transition from capitalism to socialism, the appropriate type of 'consciousness' of the working class is necessary too. Without a class-conscious working class, even if the forces have reached a certain level of development, this transition cannot take place.

How did Marx justify his 'productive force' determinism? Part of the justification, as Shaw and Cohen have pointed out is that: 'Men never relinquish what they have won ...'[45] People will not give up any productive advance they have made. Gerry Cohen justifies this thesis by reference to a further claim about human beings being inherently rational.

Secondly, as Shaw argues, when a society's forces and relations conflict, given that people do not relinquish what they have won, 'only an adjustment of the relations ... will allow society to restabilise'.[46]

Technological Determinism

This 'technological determinist' view about the connection between forces and relations has been much criticised. Critics have objected both to the adjective and to the noun. Sean Sayers, for example, objects to the adjective because, he says, it views the productive forces merely as 'machinery and techniques'.[47] But since the forces as they have been demarcated include human labour power, it is of course not true to say that the thesis that the forces are determinant entails a purely *technical* determinism. People dislike the noun because of its implied suggestion of inevitability (Sydney Hook, for one, is critical of the label 'determinism' because it appears to lead to fatalism.)[48] Critics of 'determinism' interpret it as a view to the effect that absolutely everything in society – including every human volition – is brought about by the economic. As their solution to the problem they deny the determining role of the forces of production altogether. I do not think however, that the acceptance of the view that there is a causal relation both between the forces and the relations of production and between the relations and the superstructure, has the implication that *everything* in society is determined by the economic. The more general view I think that Marx proposed, the view namely that 'consciousness' is determined by 'conscious existence', may have a different implication. Though I do not think even this position need have the offending implication, it is not this view which people have in mind when they refer disparagingly to the 'technological determinist' thesis.

What are Althusser's own reasons for objecting to the technological determinist reading of historical materialism? First of all, as we have seen, he believed that, in its economistic clothes, it stemmed from ideologies which Marx, at the time of the 'break' between his 'early' and his 'late' self, had transformed. Technological determinism, like its apparent adversary 'humanism', derived from English political economy and German idealist philosophy – ideologies which, according to Althusser, the 'late' Marx had transformed in order to produce his science of history. Both, in the end, according to Althusser, led to a form of Utopian Socialism.

Althusser in fact offers very little in the way of evidence in support either of the claim that both economism and humanism flow from common 'ideologies' or that both lead to Utopian Socialism. On the latter, he regards the 'humanist' critics of Stalinism in the French Communist Party (PCF) in the early 1960s as misguided Utopians; and he is critical of reformist 'Utopian' Marxisms, claiming allegiance to technological determinism, that see socialism as the inevitable outcome of the 'contradiction' between the developing forces of production and the constraining, fettering relations. But he nowhere argues for the necessity of these connections. As we have seen already, technological determinist interpretations of Marxism have been upheld by a Menshevik who doubted the Soviet Union's readiness, in 1917, for a socialist revolution, and by a Bolshevik who was an ardent supporter of the revolutionary change, at least in its initial stages. On the claim that economism and humanism stem from common ideologies, Althusser says that for the humanist, history is a process with a subject – Man or the working class – and an end: communism. This subject works its way, in history, Hegelian fashion, from unity, through estrangement, back to re-appropriation of the original unity. The end-state, therefore, is there at the beginning. The structure of the process is teleological. The technological determinist/economistic perspective is similarly teleological – with the productive forces in the role of 'subject'. History is the progression of the productive forces through different modes of production to their end-state: communism.

Even if one accepts, however, that each perspective has to be worked through in the fashion described (an assumption which, as we have seen, is not only questionable but false, in Bukharin's case), the parallel between the positions is tenuous. The similarity is this: each position assumes an 'agent' of change in history, and an end-state for the historical process. But on this limited characterisation, most religions would fit the bill: Christianity, where Christ's disciples fill the role of 'agent', and the second coming is the end-state; Buddhism, where the agents would be the aspirant Buddhas and the consummation 'nirvana', the hopefuls taking on the mantle of the fully fledged Buddha. Moreover, the connection of this general teleological perspective on history with the dubious 'ideologies' of political economy and German idealism is still of doubtful clarity.

A characteristic Althusserian practice is to pick the most glaring, and most unpalatable, apparent exemplification of a theoretical position, and damn the theoretical perspective because of that dubious association. So, for example, Althusser objects to 'economism' because of its connection with Stalinism.

Stalinism represented, as Althusser was to put it, the 'posthumous revenge of the Second International'.[49] Stalin's *Dialectical and Historical Materialism* was a version of mechanical materialism. It was Stalin's mechanical materialism, in Althusser's view, which was ultimately responsible for the political errors of his era.

Stalin saw history progressing, according to the 'laws' of his dialectic, through a fixed sequence of stages – primitive communism, slave society, feudalism, capitalism and socialism. The 'determining element' in this process, for Stalin, was the productive forces. Stalin's political errors, according to Althusser, were ultimately derivative from this misguided theoretical perspective. Furthermore, any failure to outline an alternative, properly scientific version of historical materialism, would be tantamount to a refusal to confront properly these political errors.

Precisely why Stalin's political mistakes derive from his misguided interpretation of historical materialism, in Althusser's eyes, is unclear. What Althusser certainly did object to, in the 'economistic' vision, is the belief, which he saw associated with it, that capitalist economic growth would bring in its train its own demise; that the 'contradiction' between the developing forces of production and the increasingly fettering relations would bring about the end, of its own accord, of the capitalist mode of production. The role of the revolutionary party, he thought, would thereby be discounted.

It is undeniable that there were 'Marxists' associated with the Second International who held this view of the transition to socialism. Whether it can be held to be even partially responsible, however, for Stalin's excesses is quite another question. Moreover, to repeat the point once more, there are 'economistic' Marxists who have not upheld the offending 'apocalyptic', self-destructive vision of the demise of the capitalist mode of production. And finally, there is no theoretical reason why 'economistic' Marxisms should lead to the 'inevitability' thesis. The 'inevitability' claim only holds if the role of the working class, and, indeed, the revolutionary party, in bringing about the appropriate change in the relations from capitalism to socialism, is denied. But there is no reason at all why the role of the revolutionary party should be left out of the picture, on the 'economistic' reading. The view, to reiterate, is that force change is necessary and sufficient, *in certain circumstances* for change in the relations. In the case of the transition from capitalism to socialism, these circumstances might and do include the role of the party. One organisation in the UK which has consistently, since its formation in 1904, adopted the technological determinist view of historical materialism, is the Socialist Party of Great Britain. This party has equally consistently attached great weight to the role of the party in inaugurating the change in 'consciousness' which it argues is additionally a necessary condition for socialist transformation.

Althusser extends his critique of 'economistic' interpretations of Marxism to claim that they ignore real history. As Gregory Elliott puts it, economism is, in Althusser's view 'analytically jejune and politically impotent ... discomfitted by the "implacable test of the facts" and therefore constantly surprised by real history – as in Russia in 1917. History's "exceptions", Althusser insisted, prove the rule of exceptionalism, being aberrant only with respect to the *abstract*, but comforting and reassuring idea of a pure, simple, "dialectical schema"'.[50]

Lenin represented, for Althusser, one of the paradigm Marxist thinkers to have respected real history, for he had attempted to produce a theoretical revision of Marx's historical materialism which accommodated the Russian Revolution. Mao, too, again in Elliott's words 'displayed exemplary sensitivity'[51] to the exigencies of real history. Althusser, therefore, used the analyses of these two 'exemplary' thinkers in the production of his own revised theory. As he put it, in *Contradiction and Overdetermination*:

> If the general contradiction (between forces and relations of pro-
> duction) is sufficient to define the situation when revolution is the
> task of the day, it cannot of its own simple, direct power induce a
> "revolutionary situation", nor *a fortiori* a situation of revolution-
> ary rupture and the triumph of the revolution. If this contradic-
> tion is to become "*active*" in the strongest sense, to become a rup-
> tural principal, there must be an accumulation of "circumstances"
> and "currents" so that whatever their origin and sense ... they
> "*fuse*" into a ruptural unity ...[52]

Every contradiction, in the true Marxist dialectic, for Althusser, is complex – an overdetermined contradiction – it is 'complexly – structurally – unevenly – determined'. In contrast the Hegelian contradiction on which the early, ideological Marx relied, is 'simple'.

This model, of complex, unevenly determined contradiction, according to Althusser, allows one to analyse the Russian Revolution, as well as the 1949 Chinese 'revolution'.

Whether or not any theoretical model is adequate to 'real history' depends, of course, on how one interprets that real history. If one has a prior belief that the Russian Revolution had something to do with socialism, or that the Maoist changes in China were along these lines, then one will want to provide an interpretation of historical materialism which accommodates these events, so interpreted. And it is yet to be proven that the 'economistic' reading of historical materialism does not allow them. But there are passages throughout the corpus of Marx's writings which suggest, I would argue, that he would not have seen alterations like that which occurred in Russia in 1917, or in China in 1949 and subsequently as having anything to do with socialism. (For more on Marx's view of the events leading up to 1917 in Russia, see below pp. 43–6). For example, in a famous passage in *Capital*, Marx says: 'Society can neither clear by bold leaps nor remove by legal enactments, the obstacles created by the succes-sive phases of its own development'.[53]

One could take this remark as applying directly to the Russian case. It is arguable that taking 'real history' into account entails not leaping to the view that every major social upheaval constitutes a case of revolution in Marx's sense.

A further point worth noting is that Althusser's description of the disjuncture between forces and relations of production as a 'contradiction' only makes any kind of sense on the deductivist, Spinozist reading of the concept of causality, a reading on which we have already, in the previous chapter, thrown some doubt.

Some Evidence in Marx for Technological Determinism

I should like to offer some textual evidence from Marx which suggests that he did adhere to the technological determinist view about major changes in history. One commentator, Miller, denies that this was Marx's view: in his view, Marx thought that major transformations are brought about not because of developments in the forces, but because they were in the interest of the ruling class at the time.[54] I will provide some counter-evidence from Marx on the subject and will interpret one of the passages Miller refers to differently from the way he does. Miller also objects that it is not true that the forces of production tend to develop autonomously.[55] And to this I would say: the forces can of course develop under the influence of the relations of production: de-skilling for example, may take place not because of any immediate alteration in the forces, but because it is in the interest of the capitalist. One effect of de-skilling may be an improvement in the forces of production. However, at some stage, a more fundamental explanation is required. One cannot appeal to the interests of the bourgeoisie as what brought the bourgeoisie into being.

In the section of *Capital* called 'Machinery and Large Scale Industry' Marx describes the effects of the introduction of machinery of various kinds into different labour processes. He points to the way in which a section of the population becomes superfluous – no longer required for the production of surplus value.[56] Here a change in the forces of production – the introduction of a machine to do the work previously performed by human labour – has the effect of altering the relations of production: the section of the workforce whose labour power was previously owned by a particular capitalist comes to stand in a different relation to that capitalist. It no longer sells its labour power to that person, so the capitalist no longer owns one of its capacities.

There are several accounts Marx provides of the relations of production altering consequent upon the alteration in the means of production and in the amount of expenditure of labour power during the Industrial Revolution. Here is one such case: 'Capital's drive towards a boundless and ruthless extension of the working day is satisfied first in those industries which were first to be revolutionised by water-power, steam and machinery, in those earliest creations of the modern mode of production, the spinning and weaving of cotton, wool, flax and silk. The changed material mode of production, and the correspondingly changed social relations of the producers...'[57]

Miller accepts that the above changes could be understood in the light I have viewed them. But he denies that the changeover from feudalism to capitalism can be so interpreted. But I think it can. In describing the change from feudal relations of production to those of capitalism, Marx remarks: 'With regard to the mode of production itself, manufacture can hardly be distinguished, in its earliest stages, from the handicraft trades of the guilds ...'[58] Miller quotes this passage as evidence that Marx did not believe that the forces of production altered with the change-over from feudal to capitalist social relations.[59] But he does not take the meaning of the last half of the sentence. The sentence continues: 'except by the greater number of workers simultaneously employed by the same individual capital.'[60] This quantitative difference in the number of people employed in the same labour process amounts to a change in the forces of production. It is certainly an alteration in the 'mode of co-operation': a feature Miller wishes to designate a productive force.

But Marx makes out that there is more than simply a quantitative change in the number of people employed, in this case: there will be, he says, 'a revolution in the objective conditions of the labour process. The buildings where the workers actually work, the store houses for the raw material, the implements and utensils they use simultaneously or in turns; in short, a portion of the means of production, are now consumed jointly in the labour process.'[61] So there is a qualitative change in the nature of the mode of co-operation.

Elsewhere Marx is, if anything, more specific on the cause of the transition from feudalism to capitalism. In the chapter of *Capital*, Vol.1, 'The Expropriation of the Agricultural Population', Marx says: 'The prelude to the revolution that laid the foundation of the capitalist mode of production was played out in the last third of the fifteenth century and the first few decades of the sixteenth. A mass of 'free' and unattached proletarians was hurled onto the labour-market by the dissolution of the hands of feudal retainers, who, as Sir James Stuart correctly remarked, 'everywhere uselessly filled house and castle ...' The rapid expansion of wool manufacturers in Flanders and the corresponding rise in the price of wool in England provided the direct impulse for these evictions.'[62]

The research of several Marxist historians confirms the above picture. Rodney Hilton, criticising Marxists' use of non-Marxist historical research tells us (against those who had assumed otherwise) that: 'Town life developed, as a consequence of the development of economic and social forces *within* feudal society, not, as Pirenne thought, as a result of the external impact of itinerant traders like Godric of Finchale.'[63] And, he says, '... surely we must see the growth of the surplus product over subsistence requirements as the necessary condition for the development of class society between the break-up of primitive communism and the beginning of capitalism. The growth of this surplus product depended of course on the development of the forces of production...'[64]

And Eric Hobsbawm says: 'A renewal period of expansion from the mid-15th to the mid-17th century marked for the first time by signs of a major break in the basis and superstructure of feudal society (the Reformation, the elements of bourgeois revolution in the Netherlands) and the first clear breakout of the European traders and conquerors into America and the Indian Ocean. This is the period which Marx regarded as marking the beginning of the capitalist era ...'[65]

These, then, are a few cases where Marx and others have pointed to changes in the relations of production being accounted for by reference to a variation in the forces.

The Russian Revolution

I believe that Marx's view on what was possible in Russia in the early twentieth century confirms this picture. According to Marx: 'No social order ever disappears before all the productive forces for which there is room in it have been fully developed.'[66]

Cohen interprets this as saying that if an economic structure perishes, then its productive potential was realised.[67] Following on from this, we can say that if the productive potential in a given society is not realised, then the economic structure did not perish. This, I wish to argue, was the position in Russia in 1917, and would have been Marx and Engels' view had they been around at the time.

An implication of this view is that 'new higher relations of production' cannot develop until the previous mode of production has developed the forces to the necessary limit. Socialist relations of production cannot appear until capitalism has matured the forces of production. It would seem to be a consequence of this that, since the forces of production were insufficiently developed, socialism could not have come about in Russia in 1917. This indeed, I believe, was Marx and Engels view on the matter. But it has been argued that they put the contrary position. P. Corrigan et al argue, in *Socialist Construction and Marxist Theory*, that one might take the passage quoted above from the *Preface* as proof of technological determinism, but this cannot be reconciled with Marx's own prognosis for revolution in such 'backward' countries as mid-nineteenth century Germany or Tsarist Russia.[68] In other words they imply that Marx contradicted himself.

Let us have a look at the literature. Perhaps the best case for the Corrigan position is a letter written by Marx to the editor of the Russian journal *Notes on the Fatherland* in 1877. There he says: 'If Russia continues to pursue the path she has followed since 1861, she will lose the finest chance ever offered by history to a people and undergo all the fatal vicissitudes of the capitalist regime.'[69] He also chastises 'his critic' for 'transforming my historical sketch of the genesis of capitalism in Western Europe into an historico-philosophical theory of the general path of development prescribed by fate to all nations, whatever the historical circumstances in which they find themselves.'[70]

And, in his letter to Vera Ivanovna Zasulich, written in 1881: 'The capitalist system is therefore based on the utmost separation of the producer from the means of production ... The basis of this whole development is the *expropriation of the agricultural producer*. This has been accomplished in radical fashion only in England. But *all other countries of Western Europe* are going through the same process.'[71] (Marx's italics) 'Hence, the "historical inevitability" of this process is *expressly* limited to the *countries of Western Europe*.'[72] (Marx's italics)

It is clear then that Marx believed that Russia need not pass through the capitalist stage of development. How does this affect the overall theory? In 1874, Engels wrote a letter replying to the Russian revolutionary, Tkascher, who believed that a revolution was not only possible in Russia but would actually be easier to carry out there than in the west; 'Only at a certain level of the productive forces of society, an even very high level for our modern conditions, does it become possible to raise production to such an extent that the abolition of class distinction can be a real progress, can be lasting without bringing about stagnation or even decline in the mode of social production.'[73] (This was published as a pamphlet in 1875).

[Russia skipping capitalism] however could only happen if before the complete breakup of communal ownership, a proletarian revolution was successfully carried out in western Europe, creating for the Russian peasant preconditions requisite for such a transition, particularly the material conditions which he needs if only to carry through the revolution.[74]

And in the Preface to the Russian edition of the *Communist Manifesto*, we read: 'If the Russian Revolution becomes the signal for a proletarian revolution in the West, so that both complement each other, the present Russian common ownership of land may serve as the starting point for a communist development.'[75]

The argument, then, is that Russia – as one individual country – need not pass through the capitalist stage of development. But any revolution in Russia could only succeed in introducing socialism there if it functioned as a prelude to world revolution. (This too was Lenin's view.)

In other words, the expression 'social order' in 'no social order ever disappears' refers to the predominant world social relations. The world as a whole could not have missed out on capitalism. Russia might; but she might only because the rest of the world had not. This interpretation is the only one consistent with Marx's overall view. Lenin was agreeing with Marx when he told us that the Russian revolution could not possibly result in socialism unless a revolution occurred in the West. Since it did not, the claim that Russia is now socialist rests on shifting sands. So, Marx's views about Russia lends support to the technological determinist picture.

Miller tells us that the technological determinist view has 'poignant implications' for such countries as South Africa and Brazil, where capitalism is pushing per capita GNP ahead by leaps and bounds, despite the most vicious povery, degradation and repression ... A technological determinist view suggests a Marxist argument against fighting for socialism now in these countries.'[76] But technological determinism is not a 'prescription' for change: it is a theory about the broad causal features responsible for major social changes.

Further evidence for the technological determinist perspective is to be found in Marx's text *Class Struggles in France*, his analysis of the revolution that took place, in Paris, in 1848.

Engels' Introduction, written in 1895, provides the clearest support for the position. First of all, Engels makes it clear that an appropriate level of development of the forces is necessary for political change: '(History) has made it clear that the state of economic development on the continent at that time (1848) was not, by a long way, ripe for the removal of capitalist production.'[77]

Marx himself confirms this position, in the body of the text. Against those who allow that historical development may sometimes 'step over' the bourgeois stage, and progress straight from feudalism to socialism, he says: 'Only bourgeois rule tears up the roots of feudal society and levels the ground on which a proletarian revolution is alone possible.'[78]

An alternative reading of the text of *Class Struggles in France* is possible, which might claim that a working class revolution did take place, and was destroyed by the legal measures of the bourgeoisie: the nascent proletarian revolution was nullified by the Republican National Assembly. This would, I believe, however, be an eccentric reading of the text, and the overwhelming textual evidence is in favour of the position I am describing. Here is one further quotation in support of my position: '... we have seen how the February republic in reality was not and could not be other than a bourgeois republic.'[79]

There is plenty of textual support from Marx, then, in favour of the technological determinist interpretation of a number of major historical changes. Where economism is seen as implying an 'economic determinism', as it is, for instance in the *Theoretical Practice* editorial quoted earlier, then Marx and Engels are economistic thinkers. On Richard Johnson's definition of 'economism', however, they are not economistic. There is no evidence that they reduce the 'dialectic of history' to the dialectic generating different production techniques, although they do hold that there is a causal link between alterations in the forces of production and changes in the relations of production. Neither are they 'economistic' on the reductionist view of it.

Conclusion

To conclude this chapter, it seems that, by some definitions of 'economism' Marx and Engels are economistic thinkers. On the other hand, support for their believing that society as a whole has causal effects on each level in it, or indeed that society as a whole is to be identified with each of its levels, is wanting. Their thinking seems to be closer to economism, in at least some of its senses, than to Althusser's structuralism.

3
Needs and Production

In the recent past, there has been a spate of 'anti-naturalist' accounts of Marx – humanist, historicist and others – that claim that Marx argued against the notion of a 'natural being'. Everything presupposed by Marx's theory – from the individuals' wants and needs to the social institutions within which people live – is supposed to be socially and historically constructed. One recent writer turns Marx into a 'deconstructionist'; he, and the French deconstructionist philosopher, Jacques Derrida, are supposed to share a common 'anti-naturalism', and 'anti-objectivism'. 'By naturalism, Marx means the effacement of history and of social geneology; something is made to seem outside the movement of time and the productive process of society.[1]

It is not only the humanists, the historicists, and the deconstructionists who decry any naturalist underpinnings there may be in Marx's writings. Even Louis Althusser, the arch anti-humanist, and, for the recent French proto-Marxists schooled in the post structuralism of Derrida and Deleuze, the crypto-positivist, does so. For him, individuals are the 'supports' or the 'effects' of the social process, and individual subjectivity is created in the 'ideological state apparatuses': the family, etc.

This 'anti-naturalist' perspective has been forcefully contested.[2] I propose to add to the number of contestants by arguing against a different area: 'constructivist' interpretations of Marx in his account of human needs and of the relation between production and needs. Rather than spending time arguing that the naturalistic perspective was indeed Marx's view, I intend to argue that the perspective makes sense of much of what Marx has to say, and that it is, indeed, true. (Norman Geras, see above, in his admirable book on the subject, has, I think, offered sufficient evidence from a variety of Marx's writings in favour of the view that Marx was indeed one sort of 'naturalist'). I propose to defend the view that there is a class of needs which preexists productive activity, and that this set of needs serves partially to explicate the notion of human beings as 'natural beings'. Just as men and women differ from other animals, so too are they, in some respects, like the birds, the bees and the monkeys. As Horkheimer and Adorno (amongst others) have argued, men and women are part of nature, and the capacities which enable them to transform nature are, at least partly, those of natural beings.

One reason I set out to defend the notion of the 'natural being' is the following: a common strand in Marxism is that communism will generate infinite capacities for the gratification of needs. Needs are limitless, and there will be, in a communist society, infinite possibilities for their satisfaction. The development of the productive forces of the capitalist mode of production has provided one of the essential conditions for the realisation of this possibility: its science and technology has offered the potential, given different class relations, for the infinite satisfaction of needs.

This often defended argument is, I believe, both irresponsible and provides a quite misleading conception of the rationale for communism. It is irresponsible because it fails to recognise the huge, and possibly irreversible damage to the ecosphere which is a direct effect of the limitless expansion of the productive forces. This can no longer be claimed to be just an effect of their use: the evidence is overwhelmingly against that.

I believe that the recognition that men and women are natural beings can exert a much needed dampener on the Marxist belief in the value of infinitely extending the productive forces, and that it can provide an alternative rationale for socialism.

I begin by considering the claim that needs are brought into being by the production process. I shall pin the argument on Althusser, not because he is the only exponent of the view, but because I think that his views are exemplary. I set out to attempt to offer the strongest possible version of the argument, so that I cannot be said to be arguing merely against a weak version of the claim. Therefore, though writers on Marx tend to concern themselves particularly with the capitalist mode of production, when presenting the view, I shall set out to generalise their argument. I shall then argue, against them, that there is a class of needs – basic needs – which exists independently of productive activity. I begin by describing Althusser's interpretation of Marx.

Althusser's View

The domain of the economic, for Althusser, covers three things: production, distribution and consumption.[3] 'Production' is a general term used to apply to the production process. A production process is described by Althusser, following Marx, as a 'labour process'; it is a process by which people labour or work to produce use-values or items to satisfy human needs. The production process can be described in material or technical terms, and labouring activity takes place in social relations. An intuitive way of understanding the distinction between a material process and a social relation would be the following: a description of someone's planting wheat seed would be a material way of seeing that 'labour process', but a description of that person as a serf performing the action for a feudal overlord would give a picture of the social relation obtaining. But according to Althusser, social relations are not reducible to relations between people; rather they are viewed as relations obtaining either between the 'agents in the production process' or between these and the 'material conditions' of the production process.[4]

'Distribution' is another general term covering two things: (a) the sharing out of people's income; and (b) the distribution of use-values produced by the production process. This second area divides into the products of *Department I*: a term Althusser (again following Marx) uses to cover those branches of production producing means of production (instruments and raw materials) and the products of *Department II*: branches of production producing consumption goods.[5]

Finally consumption: this term covers two areas – the consumption by the productive process of raw materials and the satisfaction of the needs of individuals. So there are two kinds of consumption: what Marx calls 'productive consumption' or consumption by the production process, and individual consumption.

Althusser claims that the classical political economists – who believed that needs exist before production – were wrong. Following this reading of Marx, he makes out that production determines or explains distribution and consumption. Indeed, not just consumption, but the very existence of human needs is, he thinks, determined or explained by production. Althusser explains and justifies this in the following way. Consumption, as we know, is both individual and productive. Productive consumption is consumption geared towards the 'needs' of production. It takes place during the process of production. What are consumed are the 'objects' of production – raw materials and instruments of production. Clearly the question 'Which is fundamental – human needs or production?' does not arise here because the 'needs' of production are not human needs.

Althusser says: '... the "needs" of production avoid any anthropological determination'.[6]

As for individual consumption, Althusser offers two reasons why the classical political economists' view was wrong. First, it was mistaken because individual needs are historical,[7] they change in history; and secondly, needs are recognised as such and indeed exist only insofar as they are 'effective': needs as 'effective demand' are determined by the level of income at the disposal of the individual and by the nature of the products available.

On the first of these reasons, it is not clear to me why Althusser thinks it counts as an argument against the view that needs determine production. What is biological could be changing in history, and changing independently of productive activity. And this altering biological 'nature' might explain productive activity.

Althusser's second argument looks more plausible. 'The determination of the needs of individuals by the forces of production goes even further, since production produces not only definite means of consumption (use-values) but also their *mode of consumption*, including even the wish for these products.'[8] (Althusser's italics)

'Determination' here seems to mean 'creation', since Althusser goes on to say that, 'Production produces ...' There is some ambiguity in Althusser's remarks here for he talks of Marx: '(recognising) needs in the economic function on condition that they are effective',[9] which suggests that there may be needs outside those that are expressed as effective demand. However, if this sentence is taken alongside Althusser's criticism of the relevant part of what he describes as 'classical anthropology', we have to conclude that he is making out that all needs exist as effective demand. For he wants to deny that there is a 'world of wants and needs' which underlies the economic. In other words the claim is that needs exist as what people 'wish' for, and what they wish for is expressed as effective demand. The level of income at people's disposal is an effect of the social relations of production; the technical capacities of production are responsible for the nature of the products available.[10] Assuming, then, as Althusser does, that technical capacities and social relations are features of the production process, it follows that individual consumption is determined by features of the production process.

Apart from referring to Marx's distinction, drawn in *Capital* Vol. II, between the products of 'Department I': means of production, and the products of 'Department II': means of consumption, Althusser does not spend time showing that Marx held the view he attributes to him. But he assumes that he is describing Marx's view.

Distribution, as we have seen, divides into the distribution of income and the distribution of use-values. The former, as we have already been told, refers us to the relations of production and hence to the production process. The latter is (a) distribution of means of production, and (b) distribution of consumption goods. (b) depends upon the distribution of income and leads us back to the first kind of distribution. And (a) is concerned with the exchange that takes place between capitalists and so refers us to the distribution of people into classes. Therefore, assuming that class relations are a species of social relations of production, we are led back to the production process. So distribution, in both senses, depends upon production. Althusser quotes Marx's *1857 Introduction* in support of this:

But before distribution is a distribution of the product, it is (i) the distribution of the instruments of production, and (ii) *what is a futher definiton of the same relation*, the distribution of the members of society into different kinds of production ... The distribution of the product is obviously only a result of this distribution ...'[11] (Althusser's italics)

One might set out Althusser's arguments like this:

1(a) Needs exist only as 'effective demand'.
1(b) Effective demand – or consumption – is either indivdual or productive.
1(c) 'Productive' consumption is directly dependent on the productive process.
1(d) Individual consumption depends on the level of income available and on the nature of the products one can buy and hence on the forces and relations of production.
1(e) Production takes place in relations, using forces. Forces and relations occur only here.
1(f) Hence, the existence of needs depends on production.
2(a) The distribution of goods divides into (i) the distribution of income and (ii) the distribution of use-values. (i) depends, as it does in the consumption argument, on the relations of production. So the argument is as above.
2(b) Take the distribution of means of production: this concerns exchange between capitalists, and therefore refers us to classes, and therefore, once more, to the production argument.
2(c) Take the distribution of consumption goods: this leads us back straight away, to the consumption argument.

2(d) Hence, the distribution of goods depends upon the production process.

In order to present the claim that needs are created by the production process in its strongest possible form, I must make sure that it is quite general. At the moment, it is not. The arguments, as they stand, contain premisses that are true only of the capitalist mode of production. For example, the word 'consumption' in the first argument is associated with the production of *commodities*: goods which are produced for sale on a market. And the mention of the level of income available implies that only modes of production where there are wages and therefore wage labourers are being referred to. But these problems are only terminological. One does not need to understand the term 'consumption' as applying only to commodity producing societies. And one could rephrase 1(d) to apply to alternative modes of production: the distribution of land in a feudal society determines the consumption of lords and serfs; and this distribution is determined by the relations of production. (The production process does not bring about the satisfaction of the serf's needs in quite the same way as it does those of the worker under capitalism. The serf owns his means of production, so has more control over the *nature* of the goods he produces, though probably not over the types of goods. He himself is partly responsible, in a direct way, for his potatoes and cabbages being rotten.) A similar rephrasing could be offered for a slave mode of production.

What about a socialist or a communist mode of production?[12] Here, there are no classes. The population as a whole owns the means of production (no individual or group owns them) and the whole population has democratic control over the production process. In this case, what the members of the community consume is dependent on what is produced, so it is dependent, as in that of the dominant class in other modes, upon the technical capacities of production. But there is nothing analogous to the distribution of income or to the distribution of land. People will have free access to all that is produced: they will be able to take what they want or need from the available wealth. People's consumption is dependent upon the forces of production, but not on the relations. So the conclusion of Althusser's argument is sustained, but in a weaker form.

1(a) clearly requires modifying. Some needs, for instance the need for affection or for friendship are clearly not expressed as part of effective demand. I must delimit the relevant class of needs. I suggest that the relevant class will be that class 'X needs 0' where the substituents for 0 are material or physical objects of some kind. Productive activity is, in some way or other, relevant to such needs. Thus 'X needs a car' would be relevant substitution instance, as would 'X needs food'. But 'X needs affection' would not be. And the claim here would be that those needs which have material or physical things as objects are brought into being by the production process.

So the relevant steps in the argument should be modified to say: 'needs which have material or physical things as objects'.

Clearly, desires count as part of effective demand. This does not matter. The claim is: all relevant needs count as effective demand; and not all effective demand is composed of needs of the appropriate sort.

However, even with the class of needs described as I have done, 1(a) appears to be false. There are at least two and possibly three kinds of counter-example to it.

The first is this: David, who is poor, sees me travelling around in my Cadillac. He says: 'I too want a Cadillac'. In this case the individual appears to recognise that he has the need but it does not get expressed as part of effective demand. Another similar case a Marxist might raise is: Ford car workers cannot, on my analysis, go on strike for higher wages on the basis of what they need, because what they need is expressed by what they are capable of demanding at the moment.

A second kind of counter-example is when an individual simply fails to recognise the existence of a need he or she might have. For example, a starving Indian peasant needs food, whether or not he or she recognises this and hence whether or not his or her need is expressed as part of effective demand.

Third, suppose two patients are equally badly affected by kidney disease. One can afford a kidney machine; the other cannot. It seems absurd to make the existence of the need depend on contingencies of what the two can afford.

As far as a certain class of needs is concerned – what I will call 'basic needs' – I think that the objections are sustained. But I'd just like to try to present a case against counter-examples like these counting as cases of need.

I might say: if the person does not know that he or she has the need 0 why should anyone else believe that he or she has it? What better indicator can there be for it to be true that X needs 0 than that X demands 0? The demand constitutes evidence for the existence of the need. Demand will express itself in financial terms for a certain class of needs and in other terms for other needs. The position in which one finds oneself in society determines what one can have as needs. The capitalist, who can afford an aeroplane, really does need one. The serf, on the other hand, cannot need the surplus labour of the serf because he is a serf.

The analysis of need that is emerging out of this is:

A needs X = A wants X and A expresses his/her want by demanding X.

Concerning the Indian peasant, one could say that his or her need for food will indeed be expressed as effective demand; the demand just appears as practically nought. In other words, it will count as a very low level need. And, one could say of the Ford car workers that their demand for higher wages cannot be based on a claim about what they need. It has to be founded on something else: for instance on some kind of desire. However it would be somewhat counter-intuitive for me to maintain that the one person with kidney disease really does need a kidney machine while the other person does not. The objection will be raised that, for there to be a difference in their needs, there has to be some other relevant difference than the fact that the one expresses a demand while the other does not.

A weak defence can thus be offered of the Althusserian claim, although there is at least one objection to it which I have conceded. Are there any other ways of defending the view that the existence of needs depends on production? One might say that no-one can need something which has not yet been produced: no-one in 1540 needed a washing machine. And there are certainly particular needs which are brought into being by production. Where production takes the form of capital accumulation, the need for money is created. Marx says this: 'The need for money is the true need created by the economic system.'[13]

Criticism of Althusser's Position and the Alternative

I shall now go on to argue two things against the claim I have pinned on Althusser. First of all, I propose to argue that there are some needs which do not depend for their existence on the production process. I shall do this by presenting a definition of a certain class of needs.

It has been argued that it is impossible to define needs. Kate Soper, in *On Human Needs*, quotes Aristotle with approval: 'when life or existence are impossible ... without certain conditions, these conditions are "necessary" and this course is itself a kind of necessity.'[14] She says: 'rather than condemn the circularity of his definition, we should accept it as a salutary reminder that in all attempts to argue for or against certain conditions as needs ... we are already involved in judgements about what constitutes "life" or "the good" for human beings.' She argues that needs are always relative to ends; the ends are value-laden; therefore definition is impossible.

I believe, against Soper, that it is possible to define a certain class of needs, and indeed that so doing is important for explicating the notion of a natural being.

One writer, David Miller, divides needs into three categories:

(a) Instrumental needs: e.g. Fred needs a bow in order to play the cello.
(b) Functional needs: e.g. a tennis player needs a racquet.
(c) Intrinsic needs: a starving peasant needs food.[15]

In the first case, the need is a means towards achieving an end; while in the second the need is a requirement of the carrying out of a function. The third just appears to be the statement of a need *per se*.

A further subdivision of types of need is made by Marx. Marx distinguishes 'necessary' or 'natural' needs from 'social' needs.[16] Of the former, he says: 'necessary needs (are needs of) the individual himself reduced to a natural subject.'[17] And he suggests that natural or necessary needs are needs of the person as a 'natural being'. 'Physically', he says, 'man lives only on these products of nature whether they appear only in the form of food, heating, clothes, a dwelling, etc.'[18]

Provisional examples of natural or necessary needs are these: the need for food, for a certain amount of oxygen and for maintaining one's body at a certain temperature. Another is the need for sex for procreation. They are either physiological or biological needs had by each member of the species, or they are required for the maintenance of the species. A need for shelter or for clothing would not be basic because neither is required by every member of the species.

I suggest that Marx's (and my) basic needs fall in Miller's third category of need – intrinsic needs. Most need statements are elliptical, they are usually needs in order to do something else.[19] 'X needs Y' is usually to be spelled out as: 'X needs Y in order to do Z'. In many cases of need, the Zs are ends or aims which are open to evaluation.

Does the cellist's end warrant the satisfaction of his or her need? But some need statements are not elliptical in this way; and basic need statements come into this category. Although one might spell out: 'X needs food in order to survive', the 'in order to' appears to be redundant. It is clear from the statement of the need what the end or aim is. Brian Barry gives 'A needs physical health' where A refers to a person, as an example of a need statement which is not elliptical.[20] We can spell out (see below pp. 58–9) what is meant by survival, but it is not necesssary (see K. Soper) that we do so.

One feature of basic need statements, then, is that they are not elliptical. Another is that criteria for basic needs are determinate. If an Indian peasant is starving, he or she needs food. A basic need for food must be satisfied by food. Other needs, on the other hand, are not so obviously determinate. A housewife may say she needs help from the husband with the washing, but that need may be as well or better satisfied by using a washing machine.[21]

The above are two criteria for basic need statements. I gave, as a way of spelling out the nature of a statement of a basic need: 'A needs Y in order to survive' (where A refers to a person). What counts as survival here? I take it to mean survival as a 'natural' human being. It could be taken to mean survival in a manner like Rousseau's 'natural man' who is possessed of nothing but the 'simple desires of nature'. Rousseau's 'natural man' shares the properties he has with other animals.[22] A natural being might be described as a physical or biological being.

But we require a more precise characterisation of a natural being. Superficially, we might say that a natural man or woman is that which resides in a 'state of nature': a set-up which is pre-social. But that suggestion runs contrary to Marx's view that men and women are, by nature, social beings. (See for example, the 6th Thesis on Feuerbach: 'The essence of man is not an abstraction inherent in each separate individual. In its reality, it is the aggregate of social relations.') Alternatively, 'natural' man or woman might be said to consist in the set of properties of human beings which they all share, irrespective of circumstances, historical situation and culture. But that is not right either. All human beings need some kind of social relationship, and priests can survive without sex. Being possessed by all human beings is neither necessary nor sufficient for being natural.

The analysis of need that is now emerging is as follows:

A basic need is one which must be satisfied if the individual is to survive.

If anyone would like a more detailed analysis, here it is:

(1) X has a basic need 0 = X must have 0 or X would not survive. (X refers to a person)

It appears, then, that needing is a relation between a person and an object. But this is not right, for needing is intentional. John has a need for food, whether or not there is any food around. A better proposal would be to view needing as a relation between a person and a state of affairs. So, instead of saying 'X needs food', we could say: 'X needs it to be the case that he/she has food.' Then, one could say that a need is a state of affairs such as 'X has food.'[23]

What about reference to time? I do not have a need for food just at some particular time, rather I always need a certain amount of food. I always need a certain amount of oxygen. So the account could read:

'X needs 0 basically = At all times, X needs it to be the case that he/she has 0 or X would not survive.

There are two kinds of difficulties that may be raised here. One is that it is not clear what is meant by survival. It can mean different things depending on the context. However, there is a limited conception of survial which human beings share with monkeys, lions etc., and which is not obviously value-laden at all. 'What enables it to survive' means 'what it requires in order not to die/out'. The other objection is that survival may be thought not always to be a worthwhile end.

Suppose a drug were manufactured which was necessary for survival, but which made everyone miserable.[24] It will be said that, in such circumstances, it would be better for the people not to take the drug. This raises questions I do not propose to consider here. I propose simply to take survival as a given end. Included in the notion is the idea of maximising reproductive success. Thus the need for sex, on this account, counts as basic.

The 'natural nature' of human beings is their nature as beings with basic needs. This nature is invariant in history. The idea of such a nature arouses hostility – from Marxist and non-Marxist quarters alike. Benn and Peters (as non-Marxists) have this to say:

Basic needs suggest what seems the bare minimum for a 'decent' sort of life: and this varies from time to time and place to place.

What seems the bare minimum for a decent sort of life in Britain today is a good deal more than what many Englishmen enjoyed a century and a half ago, and more too than many Asiatics enjoy today. This is important because it demonstrates the way in which the needs which we term 'basic' are relative to norms set up by different cultures ... In California creditors in a bankruptcy case can no longer place an attachment on the family television set which is now recognised as a necessity.'[25]

Setting aside the examples used – not what creditors in a bankruptcy case can do but what is necessary for survival determines what counts as a basic need – the general point needs answering. As Benn and Peters say later, in reply to Hobhouse, everyone needs food, but not everyone needs the same food: in cold climates human beings need warm clothing and shelter, in warm ones they do not. Differences in circumstances create differences in need. One cannot say, applying it to my claim, all men and women as members of a species are equal in possessing basic needs, if they are needs for different things.

For our purposes, the introduction of the concept 'equality' is gratuitous. We are not concerned, as are Benn and Peters, with the question of just distribution of goods – and we are not interested in the problem of the respects in which human beings are the same or equal. But, in reply to the main point, it is indeed true not only that the mode of satisfaction of basic needs differs from culture to culture and epoch to epoch but so, apparently, does the need itself. In a famous passage, Marx tells us: 'Hunger is hunger; but the hunger that is satisfied by cooked meat eaten by knife and fork differs from hunger that devours raw meat with the help of hands, nails and teeth.'[26] The presence of the knife and fork appears not only to change the mode of satisfaction of the hunger, but the hunger itself. Similarly, a libertarian sexual morality as opposed to prohibition, might alter the nature of sexual need itself.

However, as Marx himself confirms, both kinds of hunger are nonetheless hunger. The two hungers are, if you like, different species of the same genus. There are types of hunger ranging from that which is satisfied by pulling berries from a hawthorn bush to that which is only satisfied by a delicacy produced in a futuristic *News from Nowhere*. But all of them are hunger. What remains constant is the need for food. The type of hunger is indeed related to 'norms set by different cultures', but hunger *qua* need for food is not.

But the point might be put more succinctly: what counts as physical survival varies in history, and alters dependent upon changes in the mode of production. Basic survival for Neolithic men and women was probably pretty rudimentary. Though they might not have been subject to a lot of diseases that appear to be the product of the styles of living of advanced capitalism, they had no means for preventing epidemic diseases. And fourteenth century Britons were forced to regard the plague as a killer. Nowadays, we could ask ourselves whether getting a new heart is a basic need for someone with heart disease. What about new kidneys? If we assess what is basic here relative to the species as a whole then it would seem unlikely, unless *every* human being – or at least very large numbers of people – came to need kidney machines, that the need for a kidney machine would count as basic. Relative to the species as a whole, however, the need for propaganda against nuclear warfare might well be basic. And relative to an individual, the need for a kidney machine could be basic.

This indicates that the account needs modifying. Clearly, there is a state in history where what is required for survival is quite independent of the mode of production. Food, sex for procreation and the capacity to withstand natural disasters are the kinds of things that are necessary. If it is not caused by the mode of production, the need to be free from the plague counts as basic. But as civilisation develops, so does the need to overcome 'disasters' that are brought about by the mode of production itself. Kidney failure arises partly from the style of life under advanced capitalism; by the rich foods and drinks consumed. Hence a need for kidney machines would be a result of the capitalist mode of production. Needs such as this one are not basic precisely because they came into being as a result of the mode of production. The modification we need to introduce into the account of basic needs is this:

(2) Basic needs are those which must be satisfied to contribute to the survival of the individual.

As it stands, this characterisation lets in too much. It might be said that I need certain physiological organs, e.g. a mouth, in order to eat to contribute to the survival of the species. But these do not seem to be basic needs in the same sense as, for example, the need to eat. So I should add a clause, so that the characterisation runs as follows:

(3) Basic needs do not have as objects tools of any kind (physiological organs, machinery, etc.) They must be satisfied for the survival of the individual.

Let us compare my 'basic needs' with David Braybrooke's 'course-of-life needs'. He characterises these as 'needs such that deficiency in respect of them endangers the normal functioning of the subject of need, considered as a member of a natural species.'[27] According to him, 'The paradigms of course-of-life needs are needs that men have universally.'[28] By comparison with mine, Braybrooke's criterion is too wide in two respects: people might require love and happiness for normal functioning in contemporary Japan but not for basic survival. And the needs people have universally include some which are social: people need, quite generally, to relate to one another somehow or other.

I have now offered a characterisation of basic needs and I have met some of the objectives that will be raised against the idea of a 'natural human being'. But there are points of a different kind that Marxists will raise. To some of them, the very idea of a 'natural nature' is anathema. Thus Voloşinov, discussing Freud from a Marxist point of view, says this: 'the abstract biological person, biological individual – that which has become the alpha and omega of modern ideology – does not exist at all. It is an improper abstraction'.[29] One of his objections is to the idea of what determines what counts as a human being. He says, according to the Freudians:

... what really counts in a human being is not at all what determines *his place and role in history* – the class, nation, historical period to which he belongs; only his *sex* and his *age* are essential, everything else being merely a superstructure. A *person's consciousness is shaped not by his historical existence* but by his biological being, the main fact of which is sexuality.[30] (author's italics)

If Voloşinov means by 'what counts in a human being' what is important about him or her for political purposes, then I would agree that it is not the person's biology. If, again, he means what is essential to making that person a human being, I have already disclaimed any concern with this question. But perhaps the most important worry for him, and this is shared by critics of Timpanaro,[31] is something the latter refers to as 'biologism'. Timpanaro suggests this label might be taken to 'refer to an immediate reduction of the social to the

biological and a failure to recognise the radically new co.
made by the appearance of labour and relations of production.
respect to merely animal life ...'[32] I have nowhere tried to reduce the
social to the biological. On the contrary, I would emphasise the importance both of the social and the biological. Timpanaro continues:

> If, however, as it is too frequently the case in Western Marxism of
> our century, what is meant is denial of the conditioning which
> nature continues to exercise on man; relegation of the biological
> character of man to a kind of prehistoric prologue to humanity; ...[33]

In this case, he is not critical of biologism, and here I would agree
with him. A person's biology – in the sense of his or her basic needs –
does exert an influence on him or her. If Vološinov wishes to argue (a)
that the biological is not historical; and (b) that a person's consciousness is shaped not at all by his or her biology, then I would disagree
on both counts. What is biological is changing in history; it is
nonetheless biological and exerts an influence on human consciousness. Vološinov, if he thinks otherwise, should say why.

Critics of Timpanaro, and others, are perturbed about possible
racist and other undesirable consequences of allowing the biological
to play a significant role in historical materialism. Timpanaro says he
too is convinced that 'there does exist a danger from reactionary
biologism in the ideology of the British and still more the North
American bourgeoisie.'[34] First he suggests: 'there is a straightforward
rebirth of racist theories.'[35] The theories base themselves on the most
recent developments in genetics.

Once again, I do not believe that this criticism applies to the view
I have outlined. The supposition that there is a 'natural man or
woman' of the kind specified does not imply that there are 'natural'
superiorities or inferiorities; or, indeed, even 'natural' differences.
What I am hypostatising is possessed by human beings as a species,
and not by particular cultural or racial groupings.

There is one final difficulty concerning human 'natural' nature
and basic needs I should consider. Is it not conceivable that human
beings should cease to need to use their sexual drive in order to procreate? Artificial insemination and test-tube babies are closer than
fantasies. And, what is at the moment a more remote possibility:
might they not cease to need to eat? They might survive on pills or by
means of injections.

If the human species could survive without using the sexual drive,
then the need for sex ceases to be basic. There would still, however,

r something which allows for procreation. If it so Alth the form which procreation took was produced by the duction that would not count against the need to procre- basic. Sex was basic because it led to procreation.

at about ceasing to need to eat? So long as human beings continue to need some form of sustenance, in the form of pills or injections, they have a basic need for sustenance. Strictly, of course, the basic need is not a need to eat but a need for sustenance.

Basic needs, I suggest, could not disappear altogether without human beings ceasing to be. Radically different forms of life might be possibilities, but they would not be human life.

Furthermore, an important point is the concept of reproduction as included in the notion of production. Just as food – an object – is produced to satisfy needs, so too does the act of reproduction take place to satisfy the need to do so. Thus it makes sense to include in the concept of the 'mode of production' – or the way in which production is carried out – additionally the 'mode of reproduction', the particular manner in which reproduction takes place. It has been argued, recently, that Marx's account of 'production' is ambiguous, sometimes allowing, and sometimes disallowing reproduction. I am offering a perspective which fits with one reading of Marx, and which is, I am arguing, correct.

So, although it is true that under capitalism, for instance, the satisfaction of needs becomes merely a means serving the expansion of capital, although the worker becomes a 'being without needs' and though millions starve to death, the basic needs of sufficient numbers to ensure the survival of the species are satisfied.

But it seems that inside the capitalist mode of production the major point of production is thwarted. The potential is there for the basic needs of all to be satisfied, but they are not because the aim of production has been deflected on to profit making. Capitalism, more than any other mode of production, _disguises the nature of productive activity_.

Needs and Production

In the _German Ideology_, Marx says:

> ... we must begin by stating the first premise of all human existence, and, therefore, of all history, the premise, namely, that men must be in a position to live in order to be able to "make history".

But life involves before anything else, eating and drinking, a habitation, clothing and many other things. The first historical act is thus the production of the means to satisfy these needs, the production of material life itself. And indeed, this is an historical act, a fundamental condition of all history, which today, as thousands of years ago, must daily and hourly be fulfilled merely in order to sustain human life.[36]

Production of a very fundamental kind takes place because human beings have basic needs which require satisfaction. The occurence of acts of production is explained by the existence of such needs. Needs in general develop; and productivity changes in accordance with alterations in them. Types of hunger change, but the basic need for nourishment does not alter. It is invariant with respect to different modes of production. Acts of production gain their rationale through being geared to the satisfaction of needs. What kind of production is being referred to here? It is, of course, untrue to say that all acts of production take place for the reason I offer; so I am not abstracting out some 'essential feature' of production. However, the acts of production which are geared towards the satisfaction of basic needs are of particular significance, in two respects. First of all, the very first productive activity to take place historically was geared towards the satisfaction of at least some of the types of need I have characterised. Secondly, and just as importantly, at any point in history, production geared towards the satisfaction of the basic needs of sufficient numbers to ensure the continuity of the species must take place, or no other production could occur. Production geared towards the satisfaction of basic needs, then, occupies a uniquely privileged position. Human beings could survive without the production of televisions, motor cars or refrigerators. They cannot survive – outside Arcadia – unless some production takes place.

In feudal social relations, although the serf produces only partly to satisfy his basic needs, he does at least do this. And his surplus production does go towards the satisfaction of needs of a sort. Capitalism 'fetishises' social relations so that they appear as things; in a different way it 'fetishises' the very point of production itself, so that production is deflected from the satisfaction of needs. Just as relations between people take on 'the fantastic form of relations between things' so does production for need take on the 'fantastic form' of production for profit.

In socialism or communism production will become, once again, more like it was in its early stages. The satisfaction of needs will become its raison d'être, and the basic needs of all will be satisfied. The rationale for socialism is not based entirely therefore either on a purely technical analysis of the fate of capitalist society: the tendency of the profit rate to fall, the changing organic composition of capital, etc.; or on a moral principle of justice – the workers are exploited (though they are paid the value of their labour-power, this is less than what labour-power creates). Rather it is partly grounded on the fact that socialism will restore to production one of its central aims – the satisfaction of basic needs.

In reply to the Gotha programme, whose opening line told us: 'Labour is the source of all wealth and all culture', Marx said: 'Labour is *not the source* of all wealth. *Nature* is just as much the source of use-values ... as labour, which itself is only the manifestation of a force of nature, human labour-power.[37]

It is clear that nature is a source of use-values: the availability of natural raw materials conditions, places limits upon the use to which they can be put. But it is an extension of this point that human bio-logical nature conditions – places limits upon – the productive activ-ity of human beings. The maintenance of this biological nature is a requirement for continuing production. Men and women's biologi-cal natures have changed comparatively little over millenia. Human beings have, for centuries, been beings with a reproductive instinct, beings subject to old age and death and subject to pain and pleasure. The danger from critics of Marxism is not that they falsely describe men and women as having biological drives and instincts, but that they extend into the domain of the biological, features of human beings which are properly social. For instance, some studies on ag-gression assume as part of 'man's biological nature,' properties which are not biological at all. Marxists, in denying that people *have* biological natures are confusing the fact that some needs which some people describe as biological need not be, with a denial of the biologi-cal altogether.

So part of the answer to Althusser is that he has missed out on the one important source of wealth, in focusing entirely on production. Nature, just as much as the mode of production, determines the needs of the worker under capitalism and of the serf under feudal-ism. The availability of raw materials places limits upon the kind and the nature of productivity. But part of 'nature' is men and women's biological nature – their 'natural' needs, and these are given prior to production. Though the mode of production alters them, it does not bring them into being. Rather than production determining them, things are the other way about.

I do not wish to equate my 'basic' needs with 'man's animal nature'. This view, which stems from Descartes, is, as has been argued recently (see Benton and Midgley)[38] derogatory towards animals. Midgley shows how morally despicable behaviour on the part of humans is sometimes described as 'animal' like; and Benton points out that many ways of drawing the contrast between the human and the animal turn out to present an incorrect picture of animal behaviour. Indeed Benton argues that there is an influential reading of the late Marx, typified by Gerry Cohen's *Marx's Theory of History, A Defence* which takes the natural and non-human animal world to be merely means for the fulfilment of human purposes. In contrast, according to Benton, the Marx of the *Economic and Philosophical Manuscripts* holds a view which is much more like that of recent ecology, which is that other animals, and indeed nature itself, have intrinsic value, independent of the concerns of humans. Humans, on this perspective, are part of nature. The early Marx, however, according to Benton, remains caught up in the dualist, and 'anti-animal' perspective. For this Marx, at least on one reading, the human/animal contrast is central to the ethical critique of the alienation of labour; furthermore, human emancipation is said to involve the humanisation of nature. Benton argues that the early Marx's way of drawing the contrast between humans and animals not only gives an incorrect picture of the behaviour of most species of animals (and indeed of some aspects of human behaviour) but also that this incorrect picture serves to undermine his view of the desirability of a changed relationship between humanity and nature in communist society. Effectively, according to Benton, the early Marx claims that humanity is a species-being, in the sense that he/she 'adopts the species as his/her object', and treats him/herself as the species. Animals, by contrast, produce under the domination of immediate physical need. Benton fleshes these claims out in various ways. Summarising part of his argument: Marx meant that humans undergo development at a species level because human activity is 'free and conscious'; whilst, since the behaviour of other animals does not have these qualities, animals do not develop in this way. Benton argues that this picture of animal behaviour is inaccurate: research in ethnology reveals that animal life is diverse and complex; additionally, non-human animals interact with their environment in a variety of ways.

Benton concludes his paper by arguing that there is another naturalistic reading of some aspects of the early Marx which criticises both the dualistic contrast between humans and animals, and dualism inside the human. He argues for a reading of Marx which makes out that both animals and humans engage in the same sorts of behaviour vis-à-vis the rest of nature; humans, however, carry out this behaviour in different ways from other animals. Both humans and animals must produce to satisfy physical needs, but humans go about this process in a different way from other animals. The need for nutrition, for example, Benton argues, is common both to humans and to other animals, but the way this need is satisfied varies. For humans this need would 'ideally' be met in a way that would be aesthetically and cognitively satisfying. Indeed, the mode of its satisfaction bears on the way the need is experienced and identified.

I do not think that a dualist perspective within the human need be incompatible with the naturalistic interpretations of Marx I have defended. Drawing a distinction between a 'biological' aspect of human nature and a 'social' side need not imply that the biological side is the non-human animal. Whilst the 'social' is what is distinctively human, all that is required on a naturalist perspective, is that there are some needs – the need for food, for example – which are shared between human and non-human animals. The exact nature of these needs, their mode of satisfaction, and the way they are experienced will vary not only as between different species, but also with the level of development of the human (and possibly some other animal) species. The monkey has different needs for nourishment from the sparrow, but so do Henry VIII and Ken Livingstone. Furthermore, the level of sophistication of the individual human being will influence the way that the species's need – hunger – is experienced in any one case. Whether or not that person is a language user, for example, capable of communicating with others, will affect the extent to which the need for food is experienced as a desire for a particular type of nourishment. The human baby who only has the potential to speak, but not the capacity, does not experience any of its hunger needs as desires for meat, milk or vegetables.

Despite the variety in the identification, the mode of satisfaction and the experiencing of these needs for nourishment, they are nonetheless all instances of the one type of need. Broadly conceived, they all fall into the category I have described as 'basic'.

I would argue, however, that, in addition to these 'basic' needs, humans have other needs or desires, needs for social interaction, for example, for intellectual satisfaction etc. So described, these needs may not be unique to the human species, for other animals clearly have similar requirements. However, the fact that humans are language-users differentiates the form that needs take and their identification from those of other animals.

This is, indeed, a form of dualism, but not, I would argue, Cartesian dualism. Cartesian dualism is a dualism between humans and animals, and within the human between 'cognitive' capacities – broadly those that involve thought – and 'animal' or mechanical behaviour. The essence of the self, or the soul, for Descartes, lies on the cognitive side. This form of dualism is, as many have argued, not so much a dualism – where there is one object, the self, that has cognitive and non-cognitive aspects – but a perspective where there are two types of thing that do not interest or interconnect. Cartesian dualism is implausible, for the satisfaction of 'basic' needs, in humans, often involves the exercise of cognitive capacities. Furthermore, Cartesian dualism presents the members of the human species as though each was an independent, isolated monad or thinking thing; whereas, as I shall argue later on, social interaction is required for self-consciousness to be possible.

So Cartesian dualism is implausible. Nonetheless a dualism of types of need and forms of behaviour is, I have argued, true and compatible with Marx's naturalism.

Conclusion

I have argued, in this chapter, that one influential 'natural' interpretation of Marx on needs is wrong. Production does not 'create' all needs; on the contrary, an important class of needs pre-exists productive activity. An important class of acts of production takes place, as one might suppose, because people have needs which they must satisfy. Though capitalism does bring 'false' needs into being, even under this mode of production there are biological needs – for food and warmth, etc., which lie outside the production process, and which provide capitalist production with part of its rationale. Capitalism may have increased the technical capacity for satisfying biological needs; it may too have altered their character, but it did not bring biological needs into being. It has another rationale: the production of profit, but even production for profit requires production for need.

4
Some Feminisms and some Marxisms

Thus far, I have been defending a version of Marxism against Althusser's interpretation of it. But many feminists have argued that Classical Marxism – particularly those variations of the latter one might describe as 'economistic' – has been and continues to be, as Heidi Hartmann put it, 'sex blind'.[1] Even Marxists who have taken sex into consideration have been criticised by many feminists for seeing the oppression of women as a mere epiphenomenon of class society. Engels' writings, for example, have been described as 'economistic'. Anne Phillips, for one, said of Engels' theory that 'male power over women (is viewed) as a by-product (...of the primary division of society into classes ...)'[2] On the other hand, many 'radical feminist' writers who have reacted against this are accused of attaching insufficient weight to class. In this chapter, I intend to describe some of the arguments both against 'Marxisms' which have relegated sex to a subsidiary role, and against feminisms that have attached insufficient weight to the role of class in structuring women's oppression. This will serve to set the scene for my own attempt at an integrated explanation of the oppression of women: an account that will mesh with the interpretation of Marxism I have offered. In the chapter following, I will give more detailed criticism of one 'post-structuralist' feminist who, according to some, falls into the second of the above two categories.

The classical Marxist view is put, most famously, by Engels. In a now much criticised book he argued that: 'The first class oppression which appears in history coincides with the development of the antagonism between man and woman in monogamian marriage.'[3] The ill-treating of one sex by the other developed alongside the division of society into classes. Much of the historical background to this event, says Engels, had been the outcome of natural selection. The family altered from its 'promiscuous' form, through the consanguine version – restrictions on relations between parents and children – and through the Punaluan type – limits on siblings relating to the pairing family – out of biological convenience. In all forms of group family, while the paternity of a child is uncertain, it is known

68

who is the mother. Descent therefore is proven only in the female line, and 'mothers' are superior.

But with the acquisition of surplus wealth, individual men, according to Engels, become owners of instruments of labour and other property. They want therefore to ensure that their children inherit these acquisitions. The monogamous family is born, with the purpose of guaranteeing the undisputed paternity of the child. Napoleon's code decreed: 'L'enfant conçu pendant le mariage a pour père le mari.'[4] The supremacy of the male line is protected by 'bourgeois law'.

Oppression, however, according to Engels, is confined to relations between bourgeois partners. Amongst the proletariat, where there is no property, 'all the foundations of classical monogamy are removed.'[5] There is no means here of making male supremacy effective. Moreover, since 'large-scale industry has transferred the woman from the house to the labour market and the factory ... the last remnants of male domination in the proletarian home have lost ... all foundations ...'[6]

Engels has been frequently criticised by feminists for seeing the cause of one sex's oppressing the other to lie in the relations of production. In fact he does not see things quite like this: his claim is that the two phenomena – class society and the oppression of men by women – arose at the same time.

However, a further, now familiar feminist criticism is that sexual oppression pre-existed class societies. It cannot therefore in any major way be causally related to the existence of classes. Another criticism is that Engels' supposition, that relations between the sexes are equal and non-oppressive amongst the proletariat, is not born out by the facts. Indeed there are studies which suggest that the inequality between the sexes in the family is carried over into the workplace.[7]

There is an odd disparity furthermore between Engels' claim about the cause of oppression and his supporting reasoning. He wants to argue that class society and sexual oppression arise simultaneously. Yet he talks of the monogomous family as being encoded in 'bourgeois law'. And he says of the 'oppressed classes' that (here) 'the last remnants of male domination ... have lost all foundation.'[8] By the 'oppressed classes' here he means the proletariat. Does he think that the basis for sexual maltreatment is non-existent amongst the serfs? And how is monogamy 'encoded' amongst the feudal nobility? Or is it indeed non-existent here too? The evidence for Engels' thesis relates specifically to capitalist social relations, while the claim has to do with all class societies. Perhaps he found his thesis on the causation of oppression harder to sustain in the case of feudal society. Not wanting to deny the existence of oppression here, however, he gave ambiguous evidence about what brought it into being.

Finally we might ask ourselves: 'why should the need to secure inheritance in the male line explain all the aspects of the oppression of one sex by the other?' For instance, historically – from the Greeks on – there has been an association of rationality with masculinity. Aristotle thought that woman was 'as it were an impotent male, for it is through a certain incapacity that the female is female'.[9] As Jenny Lloyd points out: 'This intrinsic female incapacity was a lack in the "principle of soul" and hence associated with an incapacity in respect of rationality.'[10] There is no obvious link between the need to ensure the possession of property and having a capacity to reason. Working-class males have no property but their mental and physical energies, yet participation in the norms of reason is not denied to them. Locke, in the seventeenth century, had argued that it is reasonable to suppose only that some people have rights to property, and indeed rights to inheritance, but he did not equate the possession of property with the capacity to enter the house of reason. Only if the former were necessary for being rational could the required connection be drawn. And it is hard to see how such an argument could be developed.

If classical Marxism as represented by Engels has been 'sex-blind', it is argued, on the other hand, that much Radical Feminist writing has suffered a parallel fault in failing to take class and race sufficiently seriously. 'Radical' feminists have sometimes drawn on Marx's writings in their attempts to provide a materialist explanation of women's oppression. Christine Delphy, for one, sought to provide a universal explanation of women's oppression as arising out of their 'exploitation' by men in marriage.

According to Delphy marriage constitutes a labour-contract; and there exists a phenomenon she labels the 'domestic mode of production'. Inside this mode of production, women form a class: indeed, she sometimes describes them as 'productive' labourers, labourers the result of whose production are domestic services and child-rearing. In agricultural economics, women produce goods such as poultry, pigs etc., which are appropriated by their husbands for direct exchange on the market. In the industrial sphere, this does not happen in quite the same way; nonetheless men extract labour from their wives. The 'main enemy' of women according to Delphy, is not capitalism, but men as a group, in their role as husbands.[11]

Delphy's account is sometimes confusing, for instance when she variously describes 'women wives' as lying in a relationship of 'slavery', as being essentially 'proletarians' and as being involved in 'serf relations'. At times she wants to have her cake and eat it too, for example, when she is critical of Marxism while appropriating its concepts.

Many objections have been raised to Delphy's analysis. It is pointed out that women do not escape oppression merely by refusing to get married. In Delphy's defence here, she does say this: 'Since less than 10 per cent of all women over 25 are unmarried, chances are high that all women will be married at some point in their lives. Thus it can be said that effectively all women are destined to participate in these relations of production.'[12] If most women get married, some feature of the institution of marriage might explain women's oppression generally. If most women participate in the marriage contract, few of them escape its supposed 'exploitative' nature.

Yet even if she can escape this objection there are other problems with Delphy's approach. As many have pointed out, there are intractable difficulties surrounding the labelling of women as a class. Classes, on the Marxian analysis, are so defined by their relationship to the means of production. In capitalism, members of the working class own no means of production and have to sell their labour power in order to survive. Each and every member of the working class stands in this relation to the means of production. The slave is owned by the slave owner. But neither women as a group, nor married women are *defined* (except on a very eccentric view) by their relationship to the means of production; nor are they like the working class or like slaves in having to sell their labour power or themselves in order to survive. Delphy informs us that women 'produce' domestic services. But what could constitute the 'surplus' here? Maybe married women as domestic labourers work harder than is absolutely necessary for the maintenance of the family, but it is untrue to say that the husband alone benefits from this.

Perhaps the most plausible attempt to argue for the married woman's constituting a member of a class would be to draw an analogue between her role and that of the doctor. The doctor's work is not directly productive of surplus value, rather she or he services members of the workforce. Yet, on at least some definitions of the term, she or he is said to be in the working class. Married women might be said to be like doctors in respect of their servicing function, but unlike them in that they themselves benefit from their activities while the doctor does not from hers or his. The fact that the married women gain advantage might, however, be argued to be irrelevant, since most of them are not in a position to choose whether or not they perform the services. So – arguably then – they are like 'service' workers in the capitalist mode of production, and can indeed be said to form part of a class.

Notice, however, that this argument, while it might establish that if doctors are part of the working class then so are married women, does not lead to the conclusion Delphy requires: it does not generate the idea that women form a special class inside a unique mode of production.

Further, an important criticism that has been recently made by black feminists is that Delphy's model 'ignores totally the inapplicability of such a concept in analysing the complex of relations obtaining in the Black communities both historically and at present'.[13]

Finally, and ironically, it is said that Delphy's univocal analysis fails to allow for the complexities of class differences amongst women. It cannot be claimed, it is said, that all women stand in the same relationship to their oppressors. This criticism is also applied to the work of another 'radical feminist' theorist, Shulamith Firestone.

Firestone

Firestone extended Marx's and Engels' materialist conception of history to the realm of the sexual. 'Beneath the economic', according to her, 'reality is psycho-sexual.'[14] There are, she says, two basic classes: men and women; and reality conditions the economic, the ideological and other social phenomena. What, then, could correspond to the forces and relations of production within 'sexual reproductive' reality? What would count as a mode of production? And what would correlate with the class struggle? Perhaps the forces of production are replaced by the sexual organs – the 'tools' etc. And perhaps for 'modes of production' we should substitute families? Then, we should say, as the sexual organs change and develop so they come into conflict with the relations of reproduction. Implausibly we might say that the male organ grew much larger with the change to the Punaluan family and larger still with the institution of monogamy. But all this is approaching the realm of pure fantasy. Early alterations in forms of the family were in fact due partly to the simple operation of a survival mechanism and can be partially explained in terms of biological evolution, while later changes came about through the operation of social constraints.

According to Marx's and Engels' theory, the history of all hitherto existing societies has been the history of class struggle. Some of the difficulties already alluded to in relation to Delphy also apply here.

Indeed, it is perhaps more problematic to describe *women* as a class than it is to apply this designation simply to *married* women. What do women as a group produce that might constitute the surplus, to be appropriated by men as a group? There is no one thing.

Under capitalism it is in the interests of the ruling class to extract as much surplus value from the workers as possible, and one way to do this is by keeping wages low. The interests of the working class are necessarily the opposite. If we interpose Firestone's theory, however, it is only in partnerships where the one party gets satisfaction by ensuring that the other gets none, that the interests of the sexes are necessarily opposed. A further problem with her view is that it fails to distinguish *human* beings from other animals. If it is biologically caused why is there no oppression amongst the birds and bees?

Finally, Firestone's approach to the analysis of women's oppression, it has been argued, like Delphy's, is ahistorical, denying that women's procreative activities take place in a social context, one that is dominated, in Western capitalist societies, by the market. As a consequence, it is said of Firestone that, like Delphy, she downplays the significance of class differences between women, variations which affect their experiences of pregnancy and childbirth.

Similar kinds of criticism have been made of the work of Andrea Dworkin, Mary Daly and others and, as we will see in the next chapter, of the work of the French feminist, Luce Irigaray.

The Domestic Labour Debate

Given the difficulties, therefore, both with 'economistic' explanations of women's oppression, and with radical feminist theories, many socialist-feminists attempted to provide a theory linking the Marxist analysis of class with an account of the causes of women's oppression. A significant early version of such an 'integrated theory' was known as the 'domestic labour debate'. All discussants assumed a basic Marxist explanation of class exploitation. And, from Wally Secombe's and Jean Gardner's work onwards[15] contributions have mushroomed. All assumed that the family is the site of women's oppression. All argue further that the social and economic context of capitalist society (the predominant form taken by the mode of production throughout the world today) is significant in structuring the family. The form that male dominance takes on was thought therefore to be in some way dependent on historical period and social structure.

This 'domestic labour debate' brought to light the significance of women's household work. Earlier feminists, for example Betty Friedan, had written about the stifling and stultifying nature of housework particularly to middle-class American women in the 1950s.[16] But it was not until the domestic labour debate began that the importance of domestic labour in the capitalist mode of production came to be adroitly addressed. In the course of the debate, questions like: does domestic labour produce value? Is it subject to the law of value?, were raised, and various answers offered. Some argued, for instance, that women houseworkers do not simply produce use-values; labour-power is also created. In other words, women houseworkers undertake work that contributes to the production of surplus-value (see Secombe and Gardner). Critics of this view were quick to point out that the housewife as housewife does not sell her labour power as commodity to her husband. There is nothing in the relationship between husband and wife comparable to a labour-contract. The housewife is not paid a wage.[17] The issue indeed remains unresolved.

The terms of the domestic labour debate have however come in for criticism. The major criticisms feminists made of it were twofold: most of the early contributors to the discussion had argued that 'the family' exists because of the functions it fulfils in the capitalist mode of production: these functions supposedly explaining its origin. Critics claimed however, that although the relationship between privatised domestic labour and the capitalist mode of production was outlined, and sometimes described in detail, the question *why* capitalist relations developed in such a way as to ensure women's subordination was never answered.[18] Additionally, a central and fundamental reservation critics had about the debate is that its contributors failed to explain why *women* do domestic labour and as a consequence, the domestic labour debate provided no solution at all to the original problem: what causes women's oppression? Finally, one could argue that, like Engels' theory, the 'domestic labour debate' fails to explain women's oppression outside capitalism.

'Dual Systems' and 'Integrated' Theories

A further theory, most famously propounded by Heidi Hartmann[19] has become known as the 'dual systems theory'. According to Hartmann, there are two systems of domination – patriarchy and capitalism. Each has its 'oppressor' and 'oppressed' groupings, and the two are in some kind of interaction. The nature of this interraction, however, is unclear.

Hartmann argues that the introduction of the 'family wage' in the UK and the US in the late nineteenth century is one example of the way in which men came together across classes to preserve patriarchal privileges. The introduction of this wage, she implies, requires independent explanation from the development of capitalist relations of production, for these relations could have altered in different ways. There is nothing intrinsic to the logic of capital requiring this kind of development. Only by supposing that men were acting as an independent self-interested group, she suggests, can the phenomenon be explained.

But this analysis of the introduction of the family wage has been disputed.[20] It is argued, by contrast, that the family wage was a rational working-class strategy at the time, and in the interest of both men and women.

Hartmann's picture has also been criticised on the ground that its analysis of racism and ethnicism is problematic. Gloria Joseph, for one, has argued that Hartmann's analysis implies that men have come together across class, race and ethnic group divisions. But, in the US, white Anglo-Saxon men did not draw into their campaign Black or Irish men. Black men were largely excluded from the unions, so they did not benefit from the family wage. Indeed, Black male unemployment and low wages was one of the reasons why many Black married women worked in wage labour.

An alternative feminist attempt to propound an 'integrated' theory explaining both 'sex oppression' and class exploitation is that of Michelle Barrett.[21] Barrett addresses the question of the origins of women's oppression in capitalism, and alleges that the form taken by the gender division of labour in capitalism is an effect of a perdurable ideology of gender identifying childcare as women's work. The 'laws of motion' of capitalism, Barrett explains, are not 'sex blind': the separation of domestic life and work means that the respective bargaining positions of men and women in the market are markedly different. An additional factor affecting the workings of the capitalist market is that people's respective genders influence the people they are; one's gender is, as it were, etched on one's psyche.

This final point is, I believe, an important one, although what exactly it means, and why gender identity affects one's position in the capitalist labour market, are questions that still require answering.

Barrett places considerable emphasis on the role of 'ideology' in the reproduction of gender inequalities. However, she does not really tell us how gendered subjectivity – 'ideology' – comes into being. An answer to this question is surely essential if we are to say why women are oppressed.

Another interesting attempt to integrate 'Marxism' and 'feminism' is Pat Armstrong and Hugh Armstrong's *Beyond Sexless Class and Classless Sex*.[22] Summarising, their argument is: free-wage labour is a defining characteristic of capitalism, one that entails the reproduction of these labourers, to a degree, outside the sphere of the production process. Given this separation, and also the fact that women are the ones to undergo pregnancy and childbirth, women as mothers are less able to participate fully in the labour force. Because of their responsibility for domestic work, a responsibility which is, in turn, explained by their role in childbearing, women move in and out of the labour market. When women go from domestic labour to work in the factories, schools etc., the value of labour power, overall, is lowered. Women, therefore, form a reserve army of labour for this market. It is the separation between home and workplace that provides the basis for women's 'oppression' in capitalism; but it is the biological fact of responsibility for childbearing which underlines this. Armstrong and Armstrong aver that although many tasks in the capitalist mode of production are 'commodified',

> it seems likely that there are real limits to this process if capitalism, and the free wage labourer, are to continue to exist ... babies can be produced only by fertile women. Such labour, at least given present circumstances, cannot therefore be equalised and abstracted.[23]

Sex is a Marxist issue. Armstrong and Armstrong are clearly suspicious of biological accounts of women's subordination; for they say, in case anyone were to accuse them of the cardinal error of 'biologism' that: 'To recognise that women have the babies is not, however, to resort to a biological explanation of women's subordination, nor to call for the elimination of women's childbearing responsibilities.'[24]

I do not see how Armstrong and Armstrong can find egress from 'biologism' by fiat in this fashion. Their argument, after all, is that the biological fact of childbearing is ultimately causally responsible for the division in the capitalist mode of production between home and workplace. Not only can they not escape biologism, but there seems to be nothing wrong with their 'biologistic' claim. They properly accept that biology is labile. Their argument, here, is somewhat confusing. They say:

> We do not see childbearing as the same for all women or in different historical periods. We do not see biological factors as primary or even separate factors. Physical capacities do not exist outside – autonomously from – power structures and productive processes. Nor are they beyond human control and manipulation. Procreation is itself to a large extent socially constructed. It has a history.[25]

They go on to offer some interesting examples of the way in which 'production' has varied historically.

One can, however, accept that 'procreation is socially constructed' in that the experience of pregnancy, the style of giving birth, the number of pregnancies women undergo etc. are affected by such things as the standard of nutrition on offer, the availability of technological aids in childbirth and so on. But this does not entail that biological facts are not fundamental to the explanation of women's oppression. Biology may in fact only exist in social settings, but it can also be explanatorily fundamental of these setups. Thus Armstrong and Armstrong's argument seems to lead in the right direction, but they do not accept the consequences of their own view.

To conclude so far, then, I have argued that there are problems both with 'pure' Marxist accounts of women's oppression and with radical feminist explanations. Moving on to look at 'integrated' theories, I have argued that there are difficulties here as well. The last account I looked at, however, has, I believe, some fundamentally important insights, and I would like to draw on these in offering my own 'biologistic' argument, an argument which, I will suggest, is compatible with the 'economistic' Marxism defended in chapter 2.

Another Attempt

In order to explain why women have been treated unfairly, we need to point to the existence of some quality which is shared by women, cross-culturally, a property which puts them at a disadvantage. The inequality in treatment of one sex by the other cannot be explained by social or economic factors if it transcends particular social and economic situations. It cannot be comprehended by an examination of the working class exclusively or by looking only at capitalist societies because it exists outside the working class and in other places than the capitalist mode of production. This is not to say that particular strands of the oppression might not be best explained by examining capitalism or the divisions within the working class; it is to claim rather that the oppression in general cannot be accounted for by investigating these areas. It seems, then, that one obvious place to look for an explanation is biology. Men and women are biologically different. (This is different from saying that their *natures* vary.) Many of these differences[26] provide insufficient reason for an inequality of treatment. But the fact that women bear the children surely is a difference of sufficient magnitude to give rise to an inequality. Women bear children. They are also biologically fitted for rearing them for long periods during the first few months of the child's life. The mother provides the milk. These facts about the mother–child relationship, though they do not make it necessarily true that this will be the case, surely make it more likely that women will tend to have a greater responsibility than men for rearing children more generally. There are, it is true, societies where the men play as great or a greater part. And there are couples now where the man plays an equal role with the woman as 'mother'; sometimes indeed it may be the man who performs the whole of the task of bringing up a child. However rearing children makes it more likely that women will be unfitted for other tasks.

Maureen McIntosh approaches this position when she says: '... the subordination of women through an unequal division of labour in the wage sphere ... is ultimately derivative of subordination within the marriage-based household.'[27] But she does not go quite far enough. She says that 'women's performance of domestic work, especially the care of children within the home, both expresses their dependence and subordination within marriage ... and also weakens their position within the wage labour market, contributing to their low wages and poor conditions as wage workers ...'[28] As she argues, women's performance of domestic work surely does explain their subordination elsewhere, but we need to ask: why do they perform this type of work? And the answer, surely, lies along the lines I am proposing.

Rather than it being biological facts about the female members of the species *per se*, however, which lead to the inequality; I suggest that it is these matters in certain social situations. The biological data is necessary but not sufficient for the oppression of women.

Society requires that certain tasks are performed. Often, one particular group enacts them. But, clearly there need to be no connection between these two facts. Plato was surely wrong not only to suppose that people are, by nature, fitted to be warriors or rulers etc., but also in his claim that merely because many jobs must be done, one group must perform each. On the contrary, one individual could carry out a variety of roles. However, in class societies, individuals are not in a position freely to choose which class they join. And in no society (except in very rare cases) can one choose which sex to be.

In class societies, at least two things have to be ensured. On the one hand, a surplus must be produced; and, on the other, the 'producing' class must be reproduced. Given human biology, it is not surprising that these two functions have, often, in the history of capitalism been assigned to different sexes. Working-class males, male serfs etc. have 'gone out' to work; female members of the 'oppressed' classes have frequently worked in the home. Furthermore, the existence of classes – as groupings with particular tasks assigned to them – provides the motivation for giving women; as another group, a further job. In class societies, the existence of groups whose members have no choice about which one they join, is taken for granted. Here, the belief that one section of the populace is 'naturally' disposed to work, gains acceptance. Views like these belong to the ideology of such societies. Is it not very likely then, that another group will be seen as being 'naturally' fitted for another function? Given the role that the existence of certain classes performs; given the ideologies that have gained widespread acceptance and given the biological facts, a central task for women will be that of rearing children. Wherever class societies exist, there is a likelihood that this will be women's role. Undeniably, classes still exist in Eastern European countries and women retain a major responsibility for childcare in those societies. The existence of classes, then, provides a rationale, given the biological facts, for a major part of women's role being seen to be that of rearing children.

I mention class societies because it is these that assign tasks ir-revocably to particular sections of the population. It is of course true to say that any society – class-divided or not – will require work from at least some of its members. Moreover, all societies will need to reproduce themselves. Until the use of in vitro fertilisation gains widespread currency, or until human biology changes dramatically, women will bear the children. However, there would be no reason for non-class societies to assign the task of producing their goods to a particular group in society. In the absence of this there would not be the same motivation for the task of rearing children being as-signed to a particular group in society.

If we are to elaborate broad sufficient conditions for the oppres-sion of women, three factors must be brought out. First, there is the biological data. Secondly, there is the use of these biological facts in particular social set-ups and including class societies. And thirdly, there is the way this biological data is viewed in class societies – the 'ideological' factor. In a sense, then, it is true to say that in class so-cieties women are oppressed *qua* women, and not merely as work-ing class women, etc. But it is the class society which provides part of the explanation for this being true.

In a sense, like Engels, I am offering an 'economistic' version of the cause of women's oppression. I am emphasising certain relations of production along with biological facts as being fundamental to its existence. But it is an 'economism' which does not suffer from the difficulties to which Engels' theory was subject.

Nurturing their young is something that other animals do as well as human beings. Producing to satisfy their needs, on the other hand, is an activity which is distinctively human. It involves people in taking on roles which are unique to the human race. The males of the species – or anyway, a majority of them – have, on the whole, historically performed the tasks for which the human race is labelled rational. A natural link is likely to have grown up, therefore, be-tween the possession of reasoning capacities – a distinctively human trait – and being a male. The males of the species humanity by proxy represent humanity, and the women, through effectively being de-nied membership of that species are refused the attribute rationality.

Conclusion

In this chapter, I have presented, and criticised some 'sexblind' Marxisms, some feminisms that have paid insufficient attention to class, and some theories that have set out to explain both class exploitation and sexual oppression in 'integrated' fashion. I have concluded by defending the view that it is women's responsibility for childbearing, in certain social circumstances, that explains their oppression. I have outlined three conditions which, I suggest, are jointly sufficient for the explanation of women's oppression. These conditions require fleshing out, and I shall do so in the final chapter. In the meantime, however, I intend to look, in the next chapter, in more detail at the work of one so-called 'radical' feminist writer, Luce Irigaray.

5
Irigaray, Lacan and Derrida

There is a group of feminists, mainly French writers such as Hélène Cixous, Julia Kristeva and Luce Irigaray who have until recently been categorised by feminists in England, with Firestone, Daly et al. as 'essentialist' (they see oppression as arising out of an 'essence' of women) and whose work has not been seen as deserving of separate treatment.[1]

More recently, however, feminist writers in England have begun to argue that these French writers, who focus on women's *difference* from men, are not necessarily essentialist thinkers. English feminists are beginning to see that, for the French writers, the nature of the difference between women and men has been 'one of the most controversial areas of debate'.[2] The work of these French writers is therefore now beginning to be seen as deserving of discussion, in England, in its own right.[3]

I would like, in this chapter, to discuss some aspects of the writings of one of these French feminists: Luce Irigaray.

Luce Irigaray's main works, published in French in 1974 and 1977 respectively, are *Speculum*[4] and *This Sex which is Not One*.[5] In these texts she sets out to do something different from theorising the nature of 'women'. 'I can answer neither *about* nor *for* women ... it is no more a question of my making women *the subject* or the *object* of a theory than it is of subsuming the feminine under some general term, such as "women".'[6]

She would say that one cannot define 'woman', for so doing would be to conceptualise the relation between the sexes in terms of polarity and opposition, and this would be to remain caught in 'phallocentric' 'logocentric' discourse. (These terms will be explained later.) On the other hand, as Jane Gallop explains: 'Without a female homosexual economy, a female narcissistic ego, a woman in a heterosexual encounter will always be engulfed by the male homosexual economy, will not be able to represent her difference'.[7]

Women must therefore, according to Irigaray, have available to them symbolisations of their 'otherness' which are not reducible to a

82

simple definition of 'woman'. One cannot, she says, 'simply' 'keep to the outside of phallogocentrism'.[8]

Irigaray's thought owes a lot to two male French thinkers: Jacques Derrida and Jacques Lacan. Although, as Toril Moi said: 'Irigaray never acknowledges the fact, her analysis of male specular logic is deeply indebted to Derrida's critique of the western philosophical tradition.'[9] This word 'critique' is infected with the notion Derrida and Irigaray deconstruct; yet it is true that, like Derrida, Irigary offers 'deconstructive' readings of figures in the history of western philosophy. Again, like Derrida, it is *philosophical* texts upon which Irigaray focuses. Philosophy, she says, is the 'discourse that we have to challenge in as much as this discourse sets forth the law on all discourses, in as much as it constitutes the discourse on discourses.'[10] And, despite the fact that Irigaray's publication of her doctoral thesis, *Speculum de l'autre Femme*, led to her expulsion from Lacan's Ecole Freudienne at Vincennes, her work is strongly indebted to Lacan's writings. Understanding Irigaray's work, I believe, is facilitated by a knowledge of this background. I would like to preface my discussion of her work therefore, with an introduction to some relevant aspects of the thought of Derrida and Lacan.

I will begin with Derrida, focussing on his 'analysis' of a text of Jean Jacques Rousseau, both because I believe this analysis is useful for understanding Derrida, and because it concerns an area of debate that closely resembles many of the discussions Irigaray takes up on femininity.

Derrida on the Speaking Subject

In his book *Of Grammatology*[11] Jacques Derrida presents his reflections on 'being as presence' or 'logocentrism'. Derrida's 'science of writing' consists in these disquisitions. According to him, the 'logocentric tradition' (this, for Derrida, consists, as it turns out, of most of the western philosophical tradition) assumes a speaking subject, whose thoughts are clearly present to it, and whose speech reflects its thoughts. Intuitively, given this characterisation of the notion of the subject, one would have thought that the clearest example of it would be the Cartesian self. For, in the case of Descartes' subject, the speech sound 'I think' represents the thought 'I think', and the subject – the thinking subject – is 'present' as the thought to speech. Derrida, however, does not take the Cartesian self as paradigmatic of the traditions view. Instead, one central example of it, he thinks, appears in a work by Jean Jacques Rousseau: *The Essay on the Origin of Languages*. It is Rousseau's notion of the subject, rather than Descartes' upon which Derrida chooses to direct some of his attention. Derrida says: 'For purposes of this identification (discursive articulation of the logocentric epoch) Rousseau seems to us to be the most revealing.'[12] The logocentric subject is revealed through a discussion of Rousseau's views on language.

As others have pointed out,[13] it is odd, on the surface, for Derrida to have decided to take Rousseau's *Essay* to be the focal point for his discussion of logocentrism, for at least two reasons.

One is that, even in the French philosophical tradition, the *Essay* is usually taken to be marginal in Rousseau's thought; and the other is that the view of language presented by Rousseau in the *Essay* is one which challenges the received Enlightenment/Post Enlightenment view on the subject. Rousseau doubts and questions the Enlightenment view of progress. Yet it is characteristic of Derrida to take apparently marginal texts as being as important as those normally regarded as being central in the presentation of an issue. Elsewhere he chastises J.L. Austin, for instance, for setting aside 'parasitic' uses of language in favour of a discussion of 'serious' discourse.[14] Doing this, Derrida makes out, begs the question of the appropriateness of focussing mainly on non-parasitic uses of language.

But it is interesting, nonetheless, that Derrida should take as his 'target' Rousseau's *Essay*. The *Essay* argues that the vital role of language lies in the expression of feelings, cries and gestures and not, as most thinkers have argued is the case, ideas. Additionally Rousseau's view of the origin of language differs from that of most writers on the subject. Instead of claiming, as many have done, that language comes into being as a means for expressing needs, Rousseau argues that it is not needs but *passions* that give rise to the first vocal utterances: 'fruit does not disappear from our hands: we can eat it without speaking; and one stalks in silence the prey on which one would feast. But for moving a young heart, or repelling an unjust agressor, nature dictates tones of voice, cries, lamentations.'[15]

Rousseau's text is a logocentric one, for Derrida, in this sense: (a) individual units of meaning appear to be fully intelligible on their own, without recourse to any other concept; and (b) utterances seem to be meaningful directly and intuitively, without presupposing any system of utterances. One might say that a subject who feels pain or who cries is self-present to itself in a way that a thinking subject is not. The subject who feels pain is one whose 'whole essence', one might say, is revealed in the pain. There is no doubting (at least so many have argued) the fact that when I am in pain, it is I who am in pain. The feeling of pain is prior to the expression of any thought at all. Thus, arguably, the subject is present to itself in its feelings in a more immediate way than is the thinking self. For the Cartesian self must already have developed the conception of a thought and a self before it can reveal itself to itself through its thinking. One might support Derrida's view that Rousseau's *Essay* constitutes a better example of logocentrism, being-as-presence, than Descartes' *Meditations* in this way.

But there is a further reason why Derrida focusses on Rousseau in particular. Indeed Derrida would say the same sort of thing about almost any writer whose works he discusses. This is that Rousseau's text 'deconstructs' itself. It can itself be taken as an example of 'Grammatologie'. It can be seen as exemplifying 'arche writing': that sort of writing that undermines the self presence of speech. Arche writing demonstrates the play of language, the elusive substitution at work in it, that is common both to the old sense of writing and to speech.

In order to discuss Rousseau on the language of gesture, Derrida refers, additionally, to others of Rousseau's writings: *The Confessions, The Discourses* and *Émile*.

In these writings, Rousseau discusses the 'state of nature'. In the original State of Nature, for Rousseau, a hypothetical pre-social arrangement of human beings – there is no language, no separation between self and other. Needs are satisfied, but, so long as this is the case, no expressions are required to symbolise them. Yet, as some people begin to acquire property, and inequalities develop, emotions, like jealousy, begin to appear. And these emotions, Rousseau argues, require linguistic expression. At this point, a distinction between self and other begins to develop, and people begin to see themselves through the eyes of others.

Superficially, the early stage of Rousseau's thinking is not useful at all for Derrida's description of his work as logocentric. For if the self cannot distinguish itself from others, as appears to be the case in the early state of nature, then it has no sense of itself at all. But one might argue that, in a certain extended sense, the logocentric self *is* revealed in Rousseau's early state of nature. Rousseau describes the relationship between mother and child as the paradigmatically natural relationship. The child initially both identifies with and desires the mother. Hence love for another – an emotion – can be present before the child is able to distinguish itself from its mother. The emotion is present as a diffuse, generalisable 'love' which just so happens to focus on one person: the mother. Yet love for the mother is also self-love, for the child is not yet distinct from its mother. Therefore, in a certain sense, the logocentric subject is revealed here: the subject is present to itself through its love for its mother. This generalised love is both subject and object for the child: the child is itself a loving self that directs its love on itself (the mother).

This point is illustrated further. In *The Discourse on Inequality* Rousseau argues that there are two hypothetical states of nature. After the acquisition of property, described earlier, Rousseau claims that ambition rises up and instills in people desires to harm one another. When all the land has been allocated, the only way any one person can get more is at another's expense. Riots ensue. A tyrant emerges, whose driving ambition is pure greed. The people revolt and, after the period of inequality, a new state of nature with a new found equality emerges. This new state of nature, according to Rousseau, is peculiar to human beings, and in it the pre-eminent natural sentiment or virtue is 'pity'. Indeed, it is sometimes even present in the previous state of nature: 'I am speaking of compassion (pitié) which is a disposition suitable to creatures so weak and subject to so many evils as we certainly are: by so much the more universal and useful to mankind, as it comes before any kind of reflection; and at the same time so natural, that the very brutes themselves sometimes give evident proofs of it'.[16] Pity, therefore, for Rousseau, is a pre-eminently natural feeling. Natural pity, indeed: 'is illustrated archetypically by the relation between mother and child'.[17] 'Natural pity commands like a gentle voice. In the metaphor of the soft voice, the presence of the mother as well as of Nature is at once brought in.'[18]

Thus, the logocentric subject is revealed in the way I have described: through the 'natural' sentiment of pity, which is focussed, in a generalised way, by the child on the mother. This focussing on the mother is also, as I have argued, a directing on the self.

Yet one might say that Rousseau's text also 'deconstructs' itself. Pity, for him, is both supremely natural and precisely that which, by its very nature, renders culture necessary. Naturally, pity is universally directed. It is not focussed specifically on one person. In fact, as we have seen, for the child, pity is focussed exclusively on the mother, but the mother, for the child, serves to represent anyone to anyone. But pity, also, for Rousseau is that which brings about the undoing of the natural. Pity is both supremely natural, since, without it, there would be no relation between mother and child, and therefore no relations between humans at all. And yet, the specifically human expression of pity requires characteristics that take us out of nature and into culture. Rousseau argues that the *human* expression of pity requires the exercise of the imagination. The exercise of the imagination, he believes, distinguishes human beings from animals. The imagination, for Rousseau, in Derrida's words 'broaches history'.[19]

Let me expand a little, to explain Rousseau's meaning here. In a way, ideally, for Rousseau, nature should be self-sufficient. A natural state is one where all needs are provided for; desires are satisfied. And yet, for Rousseau, although in a sense the state of nature is self-sufficient, it is also lacking. How is this? Let us take the mother/child symbiosis once more to explain this notion. As I have already said, this relationship is a paradigmatically natural one. The child suckles at the breast in order to survive; the mother enables it to survive. And yet nature is lacking in several ways. First of all, some babies may (as Rousseau himself was in fact) be deprived of mothers. Another respect in which nature is lacking is that, were all the child's needs and desires to be satisfied, that would be too much for it – such a state would be, according to Rousseau, equivalent to death: 'If I had even in my life tasted the delights of love even once in their plenitude, I do not imagine that my frail existence would have been sufficient for them, I would be dead in the act.'[20] 'Pleasure itself, without symbol or supplement, would be only another name for death.'[21] Thus, were nature to allow itself free reign, that would be equivalent to annihilation. The full expression of natural emotions, for Rousseau, and pity is no exception here, leads to the annihilation of the self. But in their natural state, emotions *demand* full, generalisable expression. Thus, the natural expression of emotion is, in the end, impossible for humans, and emotions have to be expressed in other, culturally bound, ways. Rousseau's route to these culturally bound manifestations of emotion is via the imagination, which allows their symbolic expression in the absence of the actual object of the emotion.

Nature is lacking and the natural expression of emotion for humans is impossible, in further senses, for Rousseau. The mother, and nature, too, symbolised by the mother, cannot satisfy all the child's demands for she would be annihilated if she did. Thus the natural symbiosis is broken once again. And also nature is lacking in this sense: the child's love for the mother leads to self-love. When the mother fails to satisfy its demands, the child turns, as Freud was to argue, its love on itself, in the form of onanism (thumb sucking etc.).

Onanism, however, necessarily leads away from nature, since it is intrinsically symbolic: it provides constant imaginary presences. Onanism works only by imagining constant others. It therefore depends upon the possibility of symbolisation, and it leads away from nature. Finally, human beings, by their very natures, their capacities to generalise, for instance, are led away from nature. Perfectibility requires that they are. Pity, that most natural of emotions, is an emotion directed on an other. Yet, by that very token, it is not natural, since relating to another requires something that is not natural: the possibility of symbolisation. Natural pity, in fact, in the end, requires the imagination for its expression.

Rousseau's writings, then, provide an illustration of Derrida's notion and 'critique' of logocentrism. Logocentric texts, he claims, necessarily 'deconstruct' themselves. All philosophers in the western philosophical tradition are said to 'fall foul' of the notion. Derrida offers similar readings of other thinkers, showing how their thought is supposed to do so. Despite appearances to the contrary, philosophers whose views seem to be as diverse as Plato, Descartes and Husserl in fact are 'logocentric' thinkers.

By means of this reading of Rousseau's text we can illustrate the only alternative, according to Derrida, to logocentrism or 'being-as-presence', the view that 'there has never been anything but writing: there have never been anything but supplements, substitutive signifiers which could only come forth in a chain of differential references... Nature, that which words like "real mother" name, have always already escaped, have never existed; that which opens meaning and language is writing as the disappearance of natural presence.'[22]

Rousseau's pity illustrates Derrida's notion of the supplement. According to one version of Derrida's reading of Rousseau, writing supplements speech; it is added to it, it is not natural. Pity is a supplement to nature: it is an example of supplementarity in general in so far as it both adds to what it supplements (in this case, nature) and reveals an inherent lack in what it supplements. Rousseau also discusses education as a supplement to nature. Nature is in principle complete, a natural plenitude to which, as Culler puts it: 'education is an external addition'. But, Culler continues, 'the description of this supplementation reveals an inherent lack in nature; nature must be completed – supplemented – by education if it is to be truly itself: the right education is needed if human nature is to emerge as it truly is. The logic of supplement thus makes nature the prior term, a plenitude that is there at the start, but reveals an inherent lack of absence within it, so that education, the additional extra, also becomes an essential condition of that which it supplements.'[23]

In the end, as Culler argues, what Rousseau's supplements reveal is an endless chain of supplements. Writing is a supplement to speech. 'Languages are made to be spoken', writes Rousseau, 'writing serves only as a supplement to speech.'[24] The supplement is both an inessential extra, added to something that is already complete; but it is also added in order to complete that something, to compensate for what is lacking in the original. But speech is itself already a supplement: 'children', says Emile, quickly learn to use speech 'to supplement their own weakness'.[25]

For Derrida, there is no such thing as reference in language, rather all terms are essentially incomplete. Each term is a supplement to every other.

I have used this reading of Derrida on Rousseau to illustrate a number of 'central' Derridean concepts: his view of writing, his 'critique' of the notion of 'being-as-presence' and logocentrism, and his idea of the 'supplement'. As we will see, Irigaray draws on many of these notions.

I do not intend, until the end of this chapter, to say much by way of critical comment on Derrida. I will just make one point of criticism, however. This is that it is difficult for Derrida to find a route out of the logocentric tradition because, as he admits, this symbolic system is, in effect, the only one there is. So where is he writing from? Why should one accept anything he says?

Lacan

Irigaray's indebtedness to Lacan is more obvious in her writings than is her debt to Derrida. A chapter headed 'Cosi van Tuti' of *Le Sexe qui n'en est pas un* is devoted to him; her use of the term 'imaginary', which occurs throughout her writings owes much to the Lacanian 'imaginary', and the term 'Speculum' itself is partly a critique of Lacan's concept of mirror.

Like Freud, Lacan sets out to explain how individuals become human. Both assume that people are not born human, rather they become so through incorporation in the cultural order. Lacan registers Freud's break with psychologies based on humanist categories: '... as a result of [Freud's] discovery the very centre of the human being was no longer to be found at the place assigned to it by a whole humanist tradition.'[26]

He develops a critique of the Freudian theory of the Ego. Freud's first picture of the Ego has it representing the external world; the Ego controls the limitless demands of the individual's libido for satisfaction. The Ego is, therefore, a force that curtails primarily biological drives. Freud upholds this view as early as the time of writing of the largely determinist text: *Project for a Scientific Discovery*, published in 1895.[27] With the publication in 1914, of his paper *On Narcissism*,[28] however, Freud alters his view somewhat to claim that the Ego can itself be the focus for libidinal drives; indeed that it is the primary locus of these drives. Additionally, for Freud, personal identity comes to be seen as something that develops. 'A unity comparable to the ego cannot exist in the individual from the start; the ego has to be developed.'[29] Ego-libido, (energy focussed on the self) is transferred, in this process of change, onto object-libido. But as more libido is invested in the object, the more impoverished becomes the Ego. To counter this, the Ego chooses to model itself on itself. In the *Ego and the Id*, Freud argues that the Ego is a bodily ego, 'the ego is first and foremost a bodily ego.'[30] Freud expands on this: 'the ego is ultimately derived from bodily sensations, chiefly from those springing from the surface of the body. It may thus be regarded as a mental projection of the surface of the body besides representing the superficies of the mental apparatus.' Freud continues to argue, however, that the Ego has special access to external reality.

This view of the Ego is explicitly rejected by Lacan. Self-identity, for him, is an alienating, imaginary process. In his 1936 essay: *The Mirror Stage as Formative of the function of the I as revealed in psychoanalytic experience*,[31] Lacan reformulates some Hegelian concepts in his account of the formation of the Ego. This re-writing of Hegel expresses the fundamental difference between the thought of Lacan on the subject and that of Freud. Lacan tends to reject the 'biologistic' aspects of Freud's thought, and to emphasise, rather, a reading of mental life much more akin to the hermeneutic notion of 'interpretative understanding'. He would argue, for example, that no biological event can have an unmediated effect on the formation of the subject, because the influence of this event depends on the way in which it is interpreted, and this in turn is conditioned by the inter-subjective relations into which the subject enters.

Drawing on Hegel's Master–Slave dialectic, in the *Phenomonology of Mind*,[32] Lacan argues that it is only through the recognition of the desire of the other that the self gains a sense of self. Self-consciousness, according to Hegel, emerges out of the cycle of desire and its satisfaction. To crave an ice cream, for example, is to experience oneself as lacking that ice cream. The satisfaction of the desire by the consumption of the ice cream reinforces the sense of self. Yet physical objects cannot perform this role in abiding fashion, for the satisfaction of the craving obliterates the 'lack' which gave rise to the sense of self. Only, Hegel argues, when desire is focussed on another similarly placed subject, can the awareness of self properly emerge. Thus, the self gains a sense of self through the medium of the other's desire.

Using this Hegelian dialectic, Lacan describes the beginnings of the formation of subjectivity on the part of the child. He invites us to imagine the child contemplating itself in a mirror. He describes how we see it begin to develop an integrated self image. The child, who is still uncoordinated – he describes it as 'hommelette', employing the idea of the fluidity of an omelette, and that of a 'little man', a 'homme-lette' – finds reflected back onto itself in the mirror, a unified image of itself, a Gestalt. It arrives at a sense of itself as whole narcissistically, by means of an object outside it that is reflected back to it. Here is Lacan: 'We have only to understand the mirror stage as an *identification*, in the full sense that analysis gives to the term, namely the transformation that takes place in the subject when he assumes an image ...'[33] The object is both part of ourselves – we identify with it, and alien to us. Lacan refers to paintings of Hieronymous Bosch to express the uncoordinated state of the child. In spite of its being merely a mass of limbs, it gains a sense of itself as whole and unified by means of its specular image. Again to quote Lacan: 'This jubilant assumption of his specular image by the child at the *infans* stage, still sunk in his motor incapacity and nursling independence, would seem to exhibit in an exemplary situation the symbolic matrix in which the I is precipitated in a primordial form ...'[34] The mirror image is thus a misrecognition (méconaissance) of the self – the child thinks of itself as whole and unified, but this sense of self is essentially an alienated, distorted one.

For Lacan, the gaining of a sense of self is inseparable ultimately from the acquisition of language. Outside 'discourse' there is no self, even an alienated, distorted self. The child acquires a sense of itself as whole and unified as it 'enters' language.

In this context, the influence on Lacan is the structuralism of Saussure. This influence emerges most clearly in the 1955 *Discours de Rome*.[35] Saussure's claim that the relation between signifier and signified is an arbitrary one and that meaning is determined by the relations between signs (see chapter 2) profoundly affected Lacan.

Here he is: 'The first network, that of the signifier, is the synchronic structure of the language material in so far as in that structure each element assumes its precise function by being different from the others.' And 'the unity of signification, proves never to be resolved into a pure indication of the real, but always refers back to another signification. That is to say, the signification is realised only on the basis of a grasp of things in their totality.'[36] The identification of external objects, therefore, will depend upon the interpretation of signs given by speaking subjects. But Lacan also accepts the Saussurean point that language is not reducible to the utterances of members of a speech community: these utterances, we remember, Saussure labelled 'parole'. Saussure's 'langue' is the symbolic system which exists independently of speaking subjects. Having accepted this Saussurean point, Lacan must theorise the relation between this linguistic system and speaking subjects. In order to do this, he introduces a distinction between the 'Other' and the 'other'. The 'other' is the person who appears to me, in my linguistic (and other) communion with her. The Other is that person as she 'truly' is. For example, what I hear you say may not be what you really mean. However, Lacan claims in the end that the real absolutely unattainable 'Other' is language – the symbolic system – itself. We think we have access, in our linguistic communication, to 'language' – the symbolic system itself – but in fact all that we are ever acquainted with is the utterances of subjects: la parole. La Langue remains ever inaccessible.

Whereas Freud drew on biology and neurophysiology, Lacan draws on Hegel and structuralism. Yet he accepts some basic Freudian categories. He re-theorises the Freudian Oedipus complex. How does he do this? Again, like Hegel, Lacan begins this re-theorisation with the experience of physical need. He argues that as the child begins to acquire language, so she separates herself from her need. The need is expressed as a demand. But, in the demand, much is left behind, unarticulable and unsatisfiable. One can never, Lacan argues, demand what one really wants. The child, in demanding an object, has focussed his pleasure on an imaginary object. According to Lacan, what is left over from the demand that is impossible to fulfill becomes the unobtainable 'object of desire'. For Lacan, it is through this splitting between demand and need that the unconscious is formed.

This split between need and demand is one 'stage' in the progress towards humanity. Lacan's re-reading of the Oedipal dramas represents another 'stage'. As Dews puts it:

The key to [Lacan's] re-interpretation [of Freud] is [his] theory of the phallus, and in this context it is helpful to refer to a passage of [Freud's] *Inhibitions, Symptoms, Anxiety*, where Freud remarks that, 'The high degree of narcissistic value which the penis possesses can appeal to the fact that the organ is a guarantee to its owner that he can be united with his mother – i.e. to a substitute for her – in the act of copulation'.[37]

Dews goes on to explain that Lacan carries this interpretation one stage further by arguing that copulation with the mother is not the real aim of the subject; rather 'this is merely an image of full mutual recognition'.[38] The phallus, in other words, symbolises Derridean presence itself, or desire. In reality, for Lacan, as for Derrida, such a signifier is impossible. Lacan theorises this 'loss' of the phallus as castration.

Lacan argues that it is through the realisation of the mother's lack of 'the phallus' that the child first confronts the reality of castration: 'The child experiences the phallus as the centre of the desire of the mother, and situates himself in different positions, through which he is led to deceive this desire: he can identify with the mother, identify with the phallus or present himself as the bearer of the phallus.'[39]

Finally, however, the child will have to come to terms with its own symbolic castration. This is equivalent to its full entry into the symbolic order.

My discussion of Derrida was uncritical. I shall leave any critical comment on him until the end of this chapter. However, I think that it will be helpful for reading Irigaray to examine a few problems with Lacan's thought at this stage..

Some Difficulties Examined

Perhaps the central difficulty with Lacanian theory is that Lacan does not explain why the phallus is the privileged signifier. We have alluded to the fact that the phallus symbolically represents a mythical state of full recognition by a pair of subjects of one another. But why should it be the phallus that does this? Lacan disclaims any simple connection between 'phallus' and penis: the one is not a device for symbolising the other, so he cannot appeal to the actual penis, or its function or symbolic role, for any part of the explanation. Might there not be other symbols that could fulfil the function of the phallus equally well? Why should not 'Love', for example, a term for a concept that expresses, in some interpretations, full mutual recognition by a pair of subjects, fulfil the appropriate function? Or may there not be other, even better, symbolic devices that would serve the role?

One explanation for the position of the phallus Lacan sometimes seems to offer is that it is the father, in fact, who intervenes to break up the imaginary pre-linguistic unity between mother and child. Thus the 'Law of the Father', the phallus, governs the symbolic order (into which the child enters when he or she leaves the sphere of the 'imaginary'). But this is to appeal to a notion of meaning which Lacan rejects. It is to assume that the phallus represents the father, or his penis, and as we have seen Lacan has distanced himself from a theory of meaning where words refer directly to objects.

In fact, Lacan's thought appears to be contradictory here. On the one hand he disavows any simple connection between words and images or objects, signifiers and signifieds; yet, on the other, he makes reference to particular objects in his explanation of the meaning of individual signs. For example, he suggests that the child first experiences castration through seeing the mother's lack of 'the phallus'. But of course she doesn't actually lack 'the phallus'; rather she lacks a penis. Lacan cannot have it both ways. He cannot both claim that the phallus bears no relation to the penis, and also argue that the child experiences castration (i.e. loss of the phallus) through an awareness of the mother's lack of the penis.

For Lacan, the female subject is always in question, because she lacks the phallus. The symbolic system creates the feminine as absent. However, one wants to ask: why does 'the feminine' feature in the symbolic system in this fashion? Why should 'masculine' signifiers play the role they do in Lacan's system? Isn't he assuming 'phallic' power in his description of the role and functioning of the phallic signifier? Additionally, Lacan's perspective brings with it further difficulties. If 'difference' is constructed or created by language, and if there is no 'femininity' outside this symbolic system, then it is not possible to struggle to alter existing inequalities by changing 'real objects' like the family, work relations etc. Only by constructing a new symbolic system could one begin to chip away at gender inequality. This, indeed, is Irigaray's project.

Irigaray

Irigaray, as we saw earlier, embraces women's difference from men. Following on Derrida's insistence, described earlier, and further articulated in *Positions*, that 'the new concept of writing simultaneously provokes the overturning of the entire system attached to it, *and* releases the dissonance of writing within speech, thereby disorganizing the entire inherited order and invading the entire field',[40] Irigaray sets out to discover 'a new concept of the feminine' which would, like Derrida's arche writing, 'overturn the entire system attached to it'. Irigaray, as we saw, denies that she is 'making women the *subject* or the *object* of a theory'.[41] 'The feminine', she says 'cannot signify itself in any proper meaning, proper name, or concept, not even that of women'.[42]

On the surface, this view sounds somewhat like the Lacanian perspective we have just described. Yet it is not adequate to say that Irigaray's 'feminine' functions merely in Lacanian fashion. Irigaray suggests that the route to a discovery of the feminine is by 'disrupting'[43] philosophical discourse to reveal its masculinism ('philosophical' includes the work of Freud and Lacan, see *Speculum*, pp. 13–129). 'Disrupting' philosophical discourse occurs in a myriad of ways of which I will mention a few. One example: the text of *Speculum* begins with Freud, it contains sections on Plotinus, Descartes and medieval mysticism in its centre, and it ends with a chapter on Plato's cave metaphor in the *Republic*, thus subverting the order of historical time. But like the quoted sections from Derrida's *Positions*, where 'deconstruction' was said not to involve a simple reversal, so too Irigaray does not simply reverse historical time in the text. Irigaray says of *Speculum*, that 'strictly speaking' it has no beginning or end. 'The architectonics of the text, or texts, confounds the linearity of an outline, the teleology of discourse, within which there is no possible place for "the feminine", except the traditional place of the repressed, the censured.'[44] 'Furthermore, by "beginning" with Freud and "ending" with Plato we are already going at history "backwards". But it is a reversal "within" which the question of women still cannot be articulated, so this reversal alone does not suffice. That is why, in the book's "middle" texts – *Speculum*, once again – the reversal seemingly disappears. For what is important is to disconcert the staging of a representation according to *exclusively* "masculine" parameters.'[45]

Toril Moi suggests that Irigaray's reversal of the historical ordering of the philosophical texts is an action which 'resembles that of the concave mirror which is the speculum gynaecologists use to inspect the 'cavities' of the female body.'[46] Moi further points out that the Speculum is a male instrument for the penetration of the vagina, but 'it is also a hollow surface, like the one it seeks to explore.'[47] Irigaray uses the technique of imitation or mimicry in her disruption of the philosophical tradition. For example, it is used to undermine the fundamental Freudian and Lacanian device: that of the self-reflection of the subject in the mirror. As we have seen, one central version of Freud's theory of the Ego is a narcissistic one – the self gains a sense of itself through the reflection of the image of his body. The Lacanian self gains an alienated sense of itself as whole and unified through seeing itself in a looking glass. Irigaray mimics the Freudian or Lacanian self looking at himself and reveals the masculinist character of both their lookings. For both see a penis or a 'phallus' when they look. As Nye argues, woman has a vital function, even in 'patriarchal' discourse. She is a blank that 'like a mirror, reflects the masculine'.[48]

Another example of Irigaray's 'disruption' of philosophical texts is the section of *Speculum* on Plotinus, where she simply presents verbatim a section of his text in order to reveal his masculinism.

In another case, Irigaray disrupts philosophical discourse by inserting the woman in mischievous fashion. In the section in *Speculum* on Descartes: *The Eye of a Man recently Dead* she says: 'what if the "I" only thought the thought of a woman.'[49] 'What if I thought only after the other has been inserted, introjected into me? Either as thought or as a mirror in which I reflect and am reflected.'[50]

What does Irigaray have to say positively about women's 'difference'?

One of the central chapters of *Speculum*, called *La Mystérique* concerns 'mystic language or discourse'.[51] She says,

This is the place where consciousness is no longer master, where, to its extreme confusion, it sinks into a dark night that is also fire and flames. This is the place where 'she' – and in some cases he, if he follows 'her' lead – speaks about the dazzling glare that comes from the source of light that has been logically repressed, about 'Subject' and 'Other' flowing out into an embrace of fire that mingles one term into another, about contempt for form as such, about mistrust for understanding as an obstacle along the path of jouissance and mistrust for the dry desolation of reason?[52]

The chapter is prefaced by quotations from three medieval mystics – Meister Eckhart, a fourteenth-century Dominican who preached to nuns, Angela of Foligno, a fifteenth-century saint, and another mystic, Rysbroeck the Admirable. According to Meister Eckart 'Woman is the most noble way to address the soul, and it is far nobler than virgin.'[53]

Medieval mystics sought hidden truths or wisdom. Often the mystery of these truths or this wisdom was that they or it couldn't be put into words – some mystics believed wisdom to be attainable by an ecstatic revelation, others thought it was by means of 'intellectual' vision. Mystics often used the marriage/love analogy to talk about the relation between the self and these hidden truths. The soul was said to be feminine.

In her chapter *La Mystérique*, Irigaray suggests that women, who have been 'the poorest in science' have been the most 'eloquent', 'the richest in revelations'.[54] She describes the male 'subject' as 'the one who speaks, sees, thinks, and thereby confers being upon himself'[55] whilst the woman (mystic?) (soul?) goes 'beyond theoretical speculation'.[56]

Irigaray, then, associates women, in this chapter, with 'unreason', 'the unconscious', 'the soul', as with something 'beyond theoretical contemplation'. The chapter appears to be somewhat different from many of the others in *Speculum*, where Irigaray is presenting woman as she appears in the eyes of the (male) philosopher whose work she is 'deconstructing'. In the Freud chapter, for example, Irigaray suggestively implies how Freud unwittingly speaks as a man; a woman for him is a man but a castrated one. In the chapter *Une Mère de Glace* which, as we have seen consists simply of passages, verbatim, from the text of Plotinus *Enueads*, woman is left to speak as Plotinus lets her speak. But in the chapter *La Mystérique*, by contrast, Irigaray appears to be speaking positively of the role of women. She appears to associate women with 'unreason', with unconscious madness and with irrationality. It is easy to criticise her, as Sayers, Segal and Moi have done, by arguing that she is colluding with anti-feminists in celebrating the very qualities of women which have held them in subjection. Perhaps we will come to this conclusion eventually, but we must not do so too quickly. For we must not forget the influence of Derrida and Lacan. We must remember that for Derrida 'scientific knowledge', 'theoretical speculation' conceived in logocentric fashion are impossible dreams. We must not forget that for Lacan the unconscious is 'structured-like-a language'. Indeed, the 'truth' for Lacan, comes to the subject from the unconscious. The ego, we must remember, for Lacan, is an agency designed to misread this truth. The truth, for example, for the baby of approximately six months old, is that he/she is a mass of uncoordinated limbs, his body is 'fragmented', it is analogous to the paintings of Hieronymous Bosch.[57] Yet the baby misreads him/herself as experiencing himself as whole and unfragmented, through taking the mirror image of his body as himself. The infant has an imaginary mastery of his body. In reality, the situation is quite different.

For Irigaray to say that women are associated with the unconscious and unreason, given these two influences, is to say that women somehow have access to a 'truth' which is closed to men. For Irigaray to say that subjectivity is denied to women is a positive claim: women do not claim the illusory subjectivity of phallocentrism/logocentrism. Women's thought lies outside the impossible sphere of logocentrism and the alienated experience of the Lacanian subject. Woman cannot fully know or understand herself because Cartesian self-certainty anyway is impossible (even Moi in her otherwise sophisticated account of Irigaray claims that Irigaray is setting out to offer a 'theory', a 'definition' of women (p. 148, p. 139 Moi). But she is not doing that. Nowhere does she try to *name* woman or to provide a theory of the feminine. Her writings, rather, map out some characteristics that have traditionally been assigned to 'woman', yet these are not the usual qualities of nurturance and care. Instead she focusses on properties associated with woman's sexuality – her possession of the 'two lips' of the clitoris. However, unlike men, women do not have any illusion that self certainty is possible. Rather the 'knowledge' they have is of a different order. But what can we say about this 'knowledge', about women's 'experience'. Can we say anything at all that is more than, as Monique Plaza put it, 'the incoherent babblings of a baby'?[58] If, as Cixous says of l'écriture féminine (feminine writing), 'It is impossible to *define* a feminine practice of writing ... for the practice can never be theorized, enclosed, encoded'[59], can anything at all be said about feminine writing, about femininity, about feminine knowledge?

Irigaray's difficulty reflects that of Derrida. As with the latter's attempt to find a route out of the 'logocentric' tradition, so too Irigaray can only escape the symbolic order from an identity acquired in it. She, and indeed anyone else, who attempts to travel the same road, is trapped by the fact that the system to be criticised is essential in forming any 'attack' on it.

Irigaray does offer positive comment on women by describing their desire: 'woman's desire has doubtless been submerged by the logic that has dominated the West since the time of the Greeks.'[60] 'Within this logic, the predominance of the visual, and of the discrimination and individualization of form, is particularly foreign to female eroticism. Woman takes pleasure more from touching than from looking ...'[61] It seems, however, that when Irigaray comes, in her more political writings, to describe, in more concrete terms, what this celebration of woman's desire amounts to, it is, at least in the short term, to a political separatism. 'But if women are to preserve and expand their autoeroticism, their homo-sexuality, might not the renunciation of heterosexual pleasure correspond once again to that disconnection from power that is traditionally theirs. For women to undertake tactical strikes, to keep themselves apart from men long enough to learn to defend their desire, especially through speech, to discover the love of other women while sheltered from men's imperious choices and put them in the position of rival commodities, to forge for themselves a social status that compels recognition, to earn their living in order to escape from the condition of prostitute ...'[62] These are only stages and Irigaray gives the now familiar Derridean qualification: 'if their aim were simply to reverse the order of things, even supposing this to be possible, history would repeat itself in the long run, would revert to someness: to phallocratism. It would leave room neither for women's sexuality, nor for women's imaginary, nor for women's language to take (their) place.'[63] But what *would* allow these things to take (their) place? We are never given the answer.

This does indeed look like just another radical feminist, separatist stance, but perhaps it is different, for Irigaray argues that a woman's sexuality is very different from a man's. A man's is instrumental; he must do something to himself. A woman's is auto-erotic; she can touch herself. And this, as Nye claims, has consequences. 'Because of this self-touching, there will be no sharp break in her thought between touch and touched, between subject and object. A woman is always in contact with herself; she is both one and at the same time two, contrasted with the male subject which takes things one by one.'[64]

This sounds exciting, as though it makes way for a non-logocentric, non-phallocentric form of discourse. At the very least, it appears to allow a form of behaviour where individual subjects, because they 'incorporate' an 'other', take the interests and desires of others into account. Perhaps, then, the positive aspect of Irigaray's thinking might be said to lie not in language but in ontology and epistemology. She implies that 'patriarchal' societies contain individuals that are fragmented, instrumentalist and individualist. Others, in their ontology, are seen merely as instruments for the satisfaction of one's own needs and desires. Irigaray's own suggested non-patriarchal ontology is rather akin to a 'collectivist' one, one which takes others as existing, needy, desiring beings in their own right. But Irigaray would not simply be proposing a 'collectivist' versus an individual ontology. Rather, her suggestion would be that the self (the female self) is intrinsically non-individualist; it is 'neither one nor two'. It would not be merely that individuals heed others as independently existing desiring beings, instead the claim would be that the woman's self is intrinsically just as much an 'other' as it is a self. The woman, like the mystic reaching out to God, or the hysteric who has physical symptoms without a physical cause, reaches out to the 'other' because 'the other' is already incorporated inside her. The female self is just as much 'other' as it is a self; the female self is object, like any other object, instead of a 'subject-self'. It gains knowledge of itself like it acquires knowledge of objects outside itself. It has no special access to itself. Like Merleau-Ponty, Irigaray would be speaking of a 'dual being' ... 'where the other is for me no longer a mere bit of behaviour in my transcendental field, nor I in his; we are collaborates for each other in a consummate reciprocity.'[65]

This might be one interpretation of Irigaray's project. However, she certainly does focus on the importance of developing a new symbolic system in order to overcome women's oppression.

Irigaray attempts to create a new language for women, by slipping through the gaps in 'phallic' discourse. The concept 'women' in fact represents for her 'otherness', that which is 'outside' the phallic specular symbolic system. In *This Sex which is not one*, Irigaray suggests that *contra* Freud, the young girl does know of the existence of her vagina. This primary awareness of her vagina, and of the 'two lips' of her clitoris, Irigaray uses as a metaphorical device to signify a different kind of language: one that privileges plurality, instead of the unity of the 'phallic' discourse. The title of her work expresses both the idea that the woman's sex/gender 'is not one', that is that it does not exist, and is not one but rather is plural, multiple. A new 'imaginary', a new 'discourse' would be like the female genitalia: plural.

One might criticise Irigaray, at this point, for positing, like Dale Spender, a 'woman's language', that is 'other' than the 'man's language', and that is ultimately incommensurable with it. As I have said of Spender, a woman's language that is incommensurable with that of the man is not of much use in the political project of convincing men of the existence of sexism, and of attempting to alter their behaviour. Does Irigaray's project suffer in similar fashion? Certainly this is not what she wants. Unlike Spender, she is not advocating linguistic separatism. For, following Derrida, she is offering a critique of 'logocentric' discourse, of language that privileges the myth of the unified Cartesian 'whole' self. Derrida used the neologism 'Difference' to articulate the rejection of this myth. In this Derridean term, differing is combined with the idea of deferring, of postponing. Irigaray, in presenting the language of 'alterity' is not offering us 'woman's' language, for, strictly speaking, there is no 'woman'. Women's essence cannot be characterised. Woman is always subject to change, and cannot, therefore, be defined. Instead, therefore, of describing 'women's language', Irigaray offers us metaphors from female morphology for the new discourse.

I remain sceptical, however. As critics of Heraclitus pointed out, long ago, the fact of change does not make definition impossible. Even if one cannot, in one sense, step into the same river twice, this does not mean that it is not possible to identify the river. Even if each woman changes out of all recognition throughout her lifetime, this does not mean that she cannot be identified as the same. She may not be a unified, whole self, but she is, nonetheless, a self, and a self that can be identified as such.

Moreover, supposing we grant that there is no 'woman', the problem of incommensurability remains. If the language of the 'other' is not 'phallic' discourse, how does one communicate with those using the latter? Moreover, there are other criticisms we must make of Irigaray's project. As Felman put it (quoted in Moi):

If 'the woman' is precisely the Other of any conceivable Western theoretical locus of speech, how can the woman as such be speaking in this book? Who is speaking here, and who is asserting the otherness of the woman. If, as Luce Irigaray suggests, the woman's silence or the repression of her capacity to speak, are constitutive of philosophy and of theoretical discourse as such, from what theoretical focus is Luce Irigaray herself speaking in order to develop her own theoretical discourse about women? Is she speaking as a woman, or in the place of the (silent) woman, for the woman, in the name of the woman? Is it enough to be a woman in order to speak as a woman?[66]

Moi argues, moreover, that Irigaray contradicts her own prescription, in her practice. Her 'prescription' is frequently for a mimicry of male discourses. But, Moi argues, often in fact she falls, despite herself, into a 'logocentric' style of writing. She argues that Irigaray's essay *Le Marche des Femmes* (in *This Sex*, pp. 165–85) where Irigaray uses Marx's categories to 'criticise' patriarchy, turns out to be a vindication of Marx's categories, rather than a disruption of them.

Finally we come down to a fundamental similarity between Irigaray's writings and the work of Firestone et al. Again to quote Moi: 'the material conditions of women's oppression are spectacularly absent from her work.'[67] Moi continues: 'But without specific material analysis, a feminist account of power cannot transcend the simplistic and defeatist vision of male power pulled against female helplessness that underpins Irigaray's theoretical investigations.'[68] Furthermore, Irigaray's perspective does not allow for the historically changing impact of patriarchal discourses on women. She writes now, like Firestone, Daly et al. as though women's lives in the twentieth century were like the lives of Rousseau's women. Despite her denial that she is defining 'women', it looks very much as though she is doing this, in failing to allow for the historical and cultural diversity of women's experience.

But there are more fundamental difficulties, I believe, with Irigaray's project, than any so far mentioned. Derrida, Lacan and Irigaray have in common a preoccupation with the relation of language and meaning to subjectivity and consciousness. And although both Derrida and Lacan are critical of Saussure, nonetheless they both accept some version of the Saussurean structuralist point that the relation between signifier and signified is arbitrary, and that signifiers gain their meaning through their differential relations with other signifiers, rather than through any direct link with the signified. Derrida claims that 'there have never been anything but supplements.' He himself, he might say, is the only true Saussurean (although really there could be no 'true' Saussurean). Lacan transcribes the Saussurian algorithm – S/s – and claims that there is no intuitive grasp of meaning, no imaginary identification with the other. Although Irigaray sets out to disrupt the 'phallocentric philosophic order of discourse', and, although this discourse is said to include that of Derrida and Lacan, yet, as we have seen, her technique of disrupting makes use of Derridean 'techniques'. The use of these techniques is dependent upon a rejection of the 'logocentric' conception of meaning. Despite her refusal to ally herself either with

Derrida or with Lacan, she depends upon their acceptance of the Saussurean view of meaning. But, as I shall now argue, this theory of meaning is fundamentally flawed.

Derrida et al. and Anti-Realism

Broadly, I believe that all three thinkers are 'anti-realists' about meaning, and that realism, by contrast, is the correct interpretation of meaning. I begin by describing some versions of realism.

There are various types of realist theory. One is a 'metaphysical realist' perspective. On this view, 'the world' is independent of any particular representation or theory we have of it. It is possible that we might be unable to represent 'the world' at all. Truth, therefore, becomes non-epistemic. As Koethe puts it: 'we might be "brains in a vat" and so the theory that is "ideal" from the point of view of operational utility, inner beauty and elegance, "plausibility", "simplicity", "conservatism", etc. *might be false*. "Verified" (...) does not imply true.'[69] The concept of truth becomes transcendent: it is a concept which allows for a sentence to be made true or false by a condition that lies beyond any actual or possible verification. The theory has the implication that a sentence may be understood although there can be no possible recognition of the circumstances which would fulfil its truth conditions.

In the view of one 'metaphysical realist', Hilary Putnam, the world and a true description of it may be different from the best possible verified theory. The world might be constantly beyond our grasp as far as the production of verified theories goes. Actual operationally verified laws in the scientific domain may fail to express the nature of the world. The view of another realist, Bhaskar, is slightly different. According to him scientific laws exist independently of the sequence of events produced by an experimenter. There might be no human beings but there would still be scientific laws.

> In (a world without science), the causal laws that science has now, as a matter of fact, discovered would presumably still prevail, and the kinds of things that science has identified endure. The tides would still turn and metals conduct electricity in the way that they do, without a Newton or a Drude to produce our knowledge of them ... In short, the intransitive objects of knowledge are in general invariant to our knowledge of them: they are the real

things and structures, mechanisms and processes, events and possibilities of the world; and for the most part they are quite independent of us.[70]

Bhaskar believes it to be a condition of experimental activity that in an experiment, the experimenter is a causal agent of sequences of events, but not of the causal law which the sequence of events enables us to identify. There is, he tells us, an ontological distinction between scientific laws and patterns of events. Constant conjunction is neither necesssary nor sufficient for scientific laws. These, for Bhaskar, are descriptions of the tendencies of things. The independent existence of things and their mechanisms for generating patterns of events is a requirement for science to be possible.

The best possible operationally defined scientific law, in Putnam's view, may fail to describe the real world. Bhaskar's view, though not incompatible with this, offers a different emphasis. He points to the independence of laws from the procedure for their testing. For him, it is a condition of the possibility of scientific activity that the scientist set out to test laws.

The two theories present different pictures of the nature of scientific change and progress. According to Putnam, it is possible that all scientific theories are false descriptions of the real world. Every theory might contain sentences all of whose subject terms refer but which are false. Putnam's theory implies a relative indifference towards present well attested scientific theories as compared with their predecessors. Einstein's theory of relativity may be in no better position than Descartes' vortex theory as far as its claim to describe the real world is concerned. In neither case do we know that the theory is true. On the other hand, Putnam's theory is compatible with the claim that Einstein's theory is closer to the truth than Descartes'. Putnam's theory, then, veers on the side of a certain amount of scepticism about present scientific laws. It allows, however, that these laws may approximate more closely to the truth than any previous law. Bhaskar's theory, on the other hand, makes it difficult for us to allow any false law in science. Scientific laws are supposed to operate independent of the activity of experimental agents. But which ones? If we suppose it to be presently well attested theories – Heisenberg over Newton, Einstein over Aristotle, that could be argued to be according undue privilege to one moment in time.

Support for Transcendental Realism

In this section, I propose to argue in favour of a form of realism. One way of arguing in favour of the thesis comes from Bhaskar, who says that the existence of an independent real world is a requirement for the intelligibility of experimental activity. Unless the world existed independently of us, experimentation would make no sense. This idea is given in slightly different form by Gaston Bachelard who makes the point[71] that the materiality of the real world – its existence independently of thought and the possibility of its appropriation by the sciences is confirmed by their practice: by their inscribing theories in experimental forms – what Bachelard calls 'phenomeno-technics'. Bhaskar's argument is challenging unless the real world existed independent of the scientist's thoughts and activity, what on earth could scientists be doing? What would be the point of their experimental pursuits? One could provide a rationale of sorts: they might be engaged in producing a more workable or more attractive picture of the world for their contemporaries. But that answer leaves much to be desired.

Bhaskar's argument is only appropriate for those areas of scientific activity where scientists are engaged in experimental activity. In other areas of science and in the case of representational systems more generally the argument does not apply. For instance, if a scientist is engaged in producing a workable hypothesis to account for some observed phenomenon – let us take as an example the facts of variation amongst species – that activity would make sense without the assumption that either the phenomenon or the entities presupposed by the hypothesis existed in the real world. But there are other arguments in favour of realism one might offer here: if the proposed hypothesis were not true or false – or supposed to be true or false – of some entity in the real world, it would not suffice to explain the phenomenon. Were the observed phenomenon merely a deductive consequence of the hypothesis, which was not independently true, the latter would not be explanatory of the phenomenon.

A second argument that is used to establish metaphysical realism is this: it is possible to quantify over a denumerably infinite domain. The truth conditions of universal statements of this kind will be given in terms of the satisfaction of a sentence by a denumerable infinity of individuals (assuming that truth is analysed in terms of 'satisfaction'). But it is impossible for us ever to establish that these conditions obtain. We must therefore distinguish the conditions for the verification of a sentence from the conditions for its truth. The world therefore, truly described, exists independent of our verified theories.

It might be said, in response to this argument, that it establishes the realist hypothesis only for sentences of this kind. Realism is presupposed by such sentences. But perhaps we can get by without them. In reply, however, we may say that whether or not they are actually employed anywhere, they are legitimate. They exist and they presuppose realism. So the realist hypothesis is vindicated.

Employing another tack about this argument, it could be argued that it is not of much use to us. If we can never grasp the truth of such sentences, we can never know whether one theory containing such sentences is better than another. So, even if we are realist on this assumption, science and other communicational activities would become irrational pursuits.

The reply here is that one theory, although not known to be true, might approximate more closely to the truth than another. So long as the concept of verisimillitude – greater approximation to the truth – can be explained and justified, the rationality of procedures employing the above sentences will have been vindicated.

Putnam, though originally a realist, later on has reneged on his realism. He argues as follows: the metaphysical realist requires that an ideal theory – i.e. a deductively closed, consistent set of sentences – on operational criteria may be false. But Putnam now argues that this cannot be. He assumes that the world can be broken into infinitely many pieces; that a theory T1 says that there are infinitely many things. T1 is consistent and has only infinite models. T1 therefore (by the completeness theorem) has a model of very infinite cardinality. He says: choose a model of the same cardinality as the world and map the individuals of the model one-to-one onto the pieces of the world. Using the mapping to define the relation of the model in the world, one gets a satisfaction relation: a "correspondence" between the terms of the model and sets of pieces of the world, 'such that the theory comes out true – true of *the world* – provided we just interpret "true" as TRUE (Sat.)'[72] (Koethe's italics) Therefore the claim that an 'ideal' theory might be false appears to collapse into unintelligibility.

But there is a reply to this which is given by Koethe. He gives two arguments against Putnam. The first reply presupposes 'internal realism': that 'earlier theories are, very often, limiting cases of later theories' and that 'theoretical terms (preserve) their reference across most changes of theory.' He suggests we take Tt-1, Tt, and Tt+1 as a temporarily ordered succession of non-ideal theories each of which

is accepted at the time on the basis of the strictest operational constraints. The referents of all the terms common to the theories are
preserved in the transition from one to another. According to the
metaphysical realist, Tt, at the time of its acceptance, might be false
of the real world. Koethe argues against Putnam that TRUE(Sat) is
an acceptable translation of 'true' only if SAT is an acceptable interpretation of 'reference'. Reference, by hypothesis, is preserved from
Tt to Tt+1 and the proponents of both Tt and Tt+1 accept it. SAT is
defined on the basis of a model of Tt, in which case, if Tt and Tt+1
are inconsistent, Tt+1 must be partially false. So in order for proponents of Tt+1 to accept the interpretation of reference as SAT and
hold that reference is preserved in the transition, they would have to
hold that Tt+1 is false. But that is contrary to the supposition that
they accept Tt+1. Therefore proponents of T1 have a basis for reject-
ing the interpretation of true as TRUE(SAT).[73]

Koethe goes on to argue, secondly, that there can be no conception of an 'ideal' theory which both suits Putnam's arguments and
which the metaphysical realist must accept.

The above refutation of Putnam depends on the view that the referents of theoretical terms are preserved across most changes of theory. This seems a plausible assumption. It is, of course, denied by
some theorists, for example Feyerabend. But Feyerabend's theory
has the implausible consequence that, from the standpoint of Einstein for example, Newton's theory is absolutely false.

Additional support for the realist hypothesis is provided by the
general view (supported in detail by a number of recent theorists of
meaning in the analytical tradition, Donald Davidson, for example)
that truth conditions are essential in the provision of a theory of
meaning. Unless one is able to provide a theory of meaning, it is
said, one is unable to explain the special properties of linguistic
symbols that enable us to use language to communicate information. Furthermore, truth conditions are themselves explained by the
notion of reference to items in the world. This latter feature, as we
will see, is denounced by the 'anti-realists' Derrida, Lacan and Irigaray.

I propose, now, to offer a more detailed account of reference,
which suggests that the same term in two different theoretical perspectives does preserve a core meaning. I shall take the natural kind
– gold, lead etc. – as an example. It might be said that if a term is to
preserve its reference across theories, then all the properties of kinds
(at least all nominal and real essence properties) must remain. This
view may be behind the claim, often attributed by non-realists to

realists, that language 'mirrors' the world. (We will see that Derrida, Lacan and Irigaray associate this outlook with 'logocentrism', 'phallogocentrism'.) This 'extreme' view about reference has been defended, from within the analytical tradition, by Colin Mcginn, following Saul Kripke.[74] According to Mcginn, the relation between real and nominal essence of a natural kind is 'rigid'. In his view, the nominal essence properties are to be reckoned along with those in the real essence as essential to the kind. The kind will instantiate all those properties in any hypothetical 'world' in which it exists. In support of the view that at least one nominal essence property of a kind is essential to it, Kripke himself had posed the rhetorical question:

> Given that gold does have atomic number 79, could something be gold without having atomic number 79? Suppose we find some other yellow metal, or some other yellow thing, with all the properties by which we originally identified gold, and many of the additional ones that we discovered later. We wouldn't say that this substance is gold.'[75]

If all of the item's properties are essential to it, it cannot lose one without ceasing to be that thing. Kripke says:

> 'Although we could say that cats might turn out to be demons, of a certain species, given that cats are in fact animals, any cat-like being which is not an animal, in the actual world or in a counterfactual one, is not a cat.'[76]

But, there is an objection to this. If one holds that for one thing to be identical with another, the two things must have the same conditions of persistence through change, then it cannot be true that all the properties which gold now has are essential to it. For amongst the present properties of gold are the following: 'possibly ceasing to be soluble in acqua regia', and: 'possibly continuing to be soluble in acqua regia'. On McGinn's hypothesis, together with this view about identity, we should have to say: 'this stuff both is and is not gold.'

On the hypothesis that having the same conditions of persistence through change is a necessary condition for identity, and allowing possible alterations to count, nothing would have any essential properties. For any one of x's properties might undergo alteration, hence, on the strong view of identity, nothing would be essential to making the thing what it is. If we want to retain essential properties, we must either reject this strong notion of identity, or disallow possible changes. Now it is surely implausible to do away with this notion of identity: identifying x and y as 'the same' through change is, surely, part of what we mean when we say they are identical. Perhaps therefore we should reject possible change: only actual changes are to count as changes in the identity of the item. The fact that gold *might* cease to be soluble in acqua regia would not count against 'being soluble in acqua regia' being essential to gold.

Let us leave this argument for a moment and try another. Part of McGinn's justification for the claim that all the properties of a kind are essential to it, is that according to him, the scientist proceeds by 'reductive identification' of the nominal essence properties with those in the real essence. He or she sets out to identify nominal with real essence properties. But this seems to be an implausible conception of scientists' procedure in the area of natural kinds. It would make the chemist's procedure too like that of the geometer. Locke, who also talked about real and nominal essences, distinguished kinds of thing whose real and nominal essence 'coincides' from those things where the two essences do not. The first sort of thing he called a 'mode'.[77] The simple mode – triangle – is nothing but those features by means of which we identify it as a triangle, that is its being a plane figure with three straight sides. The latter is its nominal and its real essence. We have a priori or 'demonstrative' knowledge in geometry, because the geometer perceives the agreement or disagreement of ideas by the intervention of proofs, for each step of which he has certain knowledge.[78]

On the other hand, according to Locke, we do not have 'demonstrative' knowledge of substantial natural kinds in chemistry, partly because of a difference between the procedures of the two disciplines. This difference in procedure explains why it cannot be true that all the properties of a substantial natural kind are essential to it. Until we have solved the problem of induction, our knowledge in chemistry is unlike that in geometry, *even when we have observed real essences.*[79] McGinn makes chemistry too like geometry. For him things are as though chemists have solved the problem of induction.

Instead of 'reductively identifying' the nominal essence properties with those in the real essence, the chemist makes hypotheses, given one set of properties, or part of one set, about the other. So only one set of properties – either those in the real essence or those in the nominal essence – are to be considered essential to the kind. Which set? There are objections – some his own – to Locke's suggestion that it is to be the nominal essence properties. So why not those in the real essence? Locke's reservations about this derive from his hostility towards 'substantial forms' and are easily answered. The real essence properties being essential does not imply, Locke notwithstanding, that they are fixed by nature, and are always the same. A particular set of properties may be essential now but not later. And it need not follow, because the possession of atomic number 75 is essential to gold, that anyone at a particular time knows that it is. Scientists might make hypotheses – knowing the nominal essence properties – about the real essence, or vice versa.

This is an argument, as far as natural kinds are concerned, for their having to preserve their real essence properties in order to preserve their identities. We thus have a clear criterion, in this case, for when we allow an alteration in properties to count as a change in identity. We allow it when, and only when, it is a change in nominal essence property.

We could argue, then, that the real essence properties, or the 'nature' of the kind constitutes the set of properties by means of which the scientist fixes the referent of the term for the kind. The term 'gold' refers to anything which shares the nature or essence of gold. Following Kripke and Putnam we can say that a sentence saying of gold that it has the properties specified will be a necessary truth, though one whose necessity was discovered *a posteriori*. And we could follow Putnam (the earlier Putnam) further and say, with him, that anything which bears the relation - having the same nature as the kind G – to G is G. So someone might refer to gold without knowing anything about its nature. Putnam offers the following schema in explaining the meaning of 'water':

> (For every world W) (For every x in W) (x is water if x bears same 1 to the entity referred to as 'this' in the actual world W1)[80]

We can explain the meaning of 'same' as 'anything that shares a real essence with the stuff we identify as water'. The real essence might be known only as 'whatever it is that is responsible for the nominal essence properties'. We might know only that the nature of water is causally responsible for water's being a liquid, but not know what its nature is.

Wherever the nature of a kind of thing is preserved across changes in theory, then, the referent of the term for the kind of thing is unchanged. So long as the real essence of a natural kind is preserved in a change from one theory to another, scientists operating from within different theories can be said to be referring to the same thing.

In other words, so long as there is a common core of predicates which both Newton and Einstein associate with the term 'mass' they can both be said to be referring to the same thing. This common core – and not the complete set of predicates which each associates with it – constitutes the meaning of the term 'mass'. If the other predicates do not enter into the meaning of the term, then Einstein can give a charitable construal of Newton; he can hold that at least some of the claims made by Newton were true. This is surely a plausible way of understanding the relationship between the two.

The non-realist philosopher, Feyerabend, argued, of relativistic mass, that the concept is a relation, involving relational velocities; whereas Newtonian mass is a property of an object and is independent of the behaviour of the co-ordinate system.[81] He says further:

> The attempt to identify the classical mass with the relativistic rest mass is of no avail either. For although both may have the same numerical value, the one is still dependent on the co-ordinate system chosen (in which it is at rest and has that specific value) whereas the other is not so dependent.[82]

Now we may agree with Feyerabend that the Newtonian can identify the mass of a body without understanding it as related to a given co-ordinate or inertial system, whereas the Einsteinean cannot do this. However, this is not at all the same thing as admitting that the Einsteinean and the Newtonian can never refer to the same thing. This would only follow on Feyerabendian assumptions about meaning. Only if we suppose that we need to know all of the properties that are held true of a thing, in order to refer to it, are we led to the conclusion that Newton and Einstein do not pick out the same thing. We can allow that the two identify the same thing – mass – so long as each holds some of the properties to be true of mass that the other does. And, broadly, Newton and Einstein share the procedures for measuring mass. In an extended sense of the term, we might say that these procedures constitute the 'real essence' of mass. Of course this is not the same as the 'real essence' of gold – it is not the underlying set of causal properties which are responsible for the qualities in terms of which mass is identified. But we could argue that 'mass', being more of an abstract entity than gold, is more like a Lockean 'mode' than like a 'substance'. The activity of the physicist, then, would become more like that of the geometer than like that of the chemist.

To conclude this section, I do not agree with Putnam's recent reneging on his realism and I do agree with Koethe's reply. I believe, moreover, that a plausible account can be provided of his assumption that the referents of theoretical terms are preserved through some alterations of theory. A realist theory of meaning, therefore, I contend, is broadly correct.

Derrida, Lacan and Irigaray and Anti-Realism

I will now go on to argue that Derrida, Lacan and Irigaray are each, in their different ways 'anti-realists'. I begin with Derrida. This time I will refer primarily to those sections of *Of Grammatology* where Derrida discusses Saussure. I'd like to preface this discussion by looking again at some of the writings of Saussure himself.

In his *Course of General Linguistics*[83], Saussure argues, famously, that languages are constituted by internal relations. He claims that we cannot define phonemes in terms of their accoustic properties – the physical properties of the sound wave. There are at least two reasons why this is so. First of all, individual phonemes occurring in one place in a word sound different from their occurences elsewhere in the word: 't' at the beginning of the word 'table', for example, sounds different from 't' in the word 'utter'. Secondly, there are enormous variations in the way words sound amongst speakers.

Saussure claimed that the linguistic system itself determines the amount of variation that is permitted. The linguistic system brings it about that certain differences between sounds are important – that some announce a change in sign.

Saussure extended this idea to the syntactic and semantic aspects of language. He claimed that the linguistic contribution of each item to the language is given by its differences from other 'bits' of the language: 'each linguistic term derives its value from its opposition to all other terms'.[84] Saussure avers that all the relationships (syntagmatic and paradigmatic*) into which each term enters with every

---

* Syntagmatic relations are those a word holds to other words, with which it can be joined in strings, for instance Alison and laughs: these two can be joined to form a sentence; whilst paradigmatic relations are those a word holds to others that could be substituted for it in the well formed unit.

other contribute to determining its meaning. Furthermore, these relations *exhaust* the meaning of each word. For example, there is nothing more to the meaning of the word 'black' than its relations with other signs.

Already we see one obvious respect in which Saussure is an anti-realist. He denies that reference plays any role at all in the meaning of any word. The meaning of the word 'black' is exhausted by its relations with other signs. But this is to forget about the contribution *of the reference to black things* to the meaning of the word 'black'.

Saussure does distinguish the *signified* (that which is signified) from the *signifier* (that which signifies). But this signified is not a language – independent referent – rather it is a concept, a thought. Moreover, the nature of this thought is determined by relations internal to the language.

As the realist claims, however, reference is crucial to capturing the difference between language, which is used to communicate, and games, like chess. The rules of chess are internal to the game, and the moves in the game occur solely in it. Although Saussure would have us believe otherwise, this is not the case with language.

There are other difficulties consequent on the structuralist rejection of reference. It is difficult for Saussure to explain developmental facts about language. Any new term introduced into the language changes the meaning of all other terms. How then does language acquistion take place?

Why, one might ask, does Saussure reject reference? Part of the answer is that he argues that linguistic signs are *arbitrary*. There is no intrinsic relation between the sign 'dog' and dogs; the word 'dog' has no dog-like qualities. Therefore, he says, the meaning of the word 'dog' is defined by its relations with other words.

Derrida and Saussure

This 'arbitrariness' of the sign is something of which Derrida approves in Saussure. He quotes, without obvious disagreement, 'the thesis of the *arbitrariness* of the sign'.[85] Where Derrida 'disagrees' with Saussure (and I use this expression recognising that it is not one of which Derrida would approve) it is not here, but elsewhere. He 'approves' of Saussure's views on the relationality of linguistic terms. But he thinks that Saussure did not go far enough. Saussure, Derrida points out, 'contests' the notion that speech 'clothes' thought.[86] Speech, in other words, Derrida is saying, for Saussure, does not represent thought. Individual words do not name or refer to thoughts. Instead, as we have seen, thoughts only exist in language. Language creates thought. But, Derrida says, Saussure continues to uphold the 'old', 'logocentric' view on the relation between speech and writing. Writing, for Saussure, as with the philosophers in the logocentric tradition before him – Plato, Aristotle, Rousseau and Hegel, to name but a few – is derivative of speech. Writing, for Saussure, according to Derrida is 'artificial exteriority', a 'clothing' of speech.[87] Writing represents speech. Saussure, just like his predecessors, mistakenly, says Derrida, takes the spoken word to be the object of linguistics.[88] Writing will be 'the outside, the exterior representation of language and of this "thought-sound".'[89] Writing, therefore, says Derrida, is the sign of a sign. Derrida is claiming, in other words, that Saussure ought to have extended his thesis about the meanings of signs to the relation between writing and speech. Just as each internal sign gains its meaning from its relations to other signs, and just as thought is nothing over and above the relations between these signs, so should writing be. Writing ought to be itself nothing but the relations between linguistic signs. But, Derrida would say, once one sees the relation between speech and writing in this fashion, then the distinction between speech and writing is undermined altogether. Speech becomes a form of writing, and writing a type of speech.

Although Saussure, therefore, according to Derrida, removes himself from the logocentric tradition with his view on the arbitrariness of the sign, he nonetheless remains caught up in it as regards his perspective on speech and writing.

Derrida has rejected yet another realist viewpoint. He concurs with Saussure's dismissal of the notion of reference, and further with his perspective on the relation between language and thought, but he adds one further dimension – the rejection of the distinction between speech and writing. Thus the criticisms articulated earlier, of Saussure, apply also in his case.

Furthermore, as we have noted, both Derrida and Saussure see thought as being characterised by language. Thought does not exist outside language. But surely this is not true. Those who are supposed to have seen abominable snowmen could have had thoughts about them without having been able to name them. Physicists, recently, in proposing the existence of new subatomic particles, had thoughts about those before naming them. Thoughts, as the realist would admit, can exist independently of language.

Also, there is something odd about the connection between the view that the relation between a term and the object for which it stands is *arbitrary*, and the claim that the meaning of every term is given by its relations to all others. Saussure, and Derrida too, appear to think that it is *because* the meanings of signs are arbitrary that there is no reference. But it could both be the case that the arbitrariness claim holds *and* that signs refer. Reference does not depend on signs being like their referents. Derrida, in bringing his accusation of logocentrism against so many writers in the history of philosophy, appears to think that it does. Derrida gives the following characterisation of the logocentric philosopher:

> if ... spoken words are the symbols of mental experience and written words are the symbols of spoken words, it is because the voice, producer of *the first symbols*, has a relationship of essential and immediate proximity with the mind. Producer of the first signifier, it is not just a simple signifier among others. It signifies 'mental experiences' which themselves reflect or mirror things by natural resemblance.[90]

Derrida is describing Aristotle, but one has a sneaking suspicion that this is his model for logocentrism.

So far, in characterising Derrida's views on language, I have referred solely to *Of Grammatology*. Yet his anti-realism is clearly articulated throughout the corpus of his writings. In 'Structure, Sign and Play', for example, in the book *Writing and Difference*,[91] Derrida says, in Saussurean vein:

> ... (this was) the moment when, in the absence of a center or origin, everything became discourse – provided we can agree on this word – that is to say, a system in which the central signified, the original or transcendental signified, is never absolutely present outside a system of differences.[92]

Derrida refers approvingly, in this paper, to Nietzsche and Freud: the former because of his 'critique of metaphysics' 'the critique of the concepts of Being and truth, for which were substituted the concepts of play, interpretation, and sign (sign without present truth),' and Freud for his 'critique of self presence, that is the critique of consciousness, of the subject, of self-identity and self-proximity or self-possession; and, more radically', he says, 'the Heideggerian destruction of metaphysics, of onto theology, of the determination of Being as presence.'[93]

As we have already seen, in the quote from *Of Grammatology*, the model of meaning of which Derrida 'disapproves' is one which has the meanings of words like Lockean ideas 'present' in the mind of the speaker as she utters the word. Once more, I reiterate, this need not be the perspective on meaning held by the realist. Not all those who believe in reference are like Descartes or Locke.

Throughout his writings, from the very early *Origin of Geometry* to recent works, we find the view of meaning affirmed. In *Glas*[94] and in *Positions*[95] (where Derrida summarises his main concernes in a very clear fashion) the preoccupation with the arbitrariness of the sign, and with the extension of this to the relation between speech and writing, remains.

Lacan

We find a similar perspective articulated in Lacan. Peter Dews, in his book *The Logics of Disintegration*, describes a shift in Lacan's thought that took place after the writing of the *Discours de Rome*. This change, he says, 'was undoubtedly in large part the result of a growing awareness of the methodological principles of structuralism'.[96]

As Dews points out, Lacan's early writings contain material which provides fertile ground for the acceptance of structuralist ideas. There is a 'strain of argument', he suggests, in *De la Psychose Paranoiaque*, where Lacan is 'anxious to deny that a semantic and psychogenic account of mental illness must entail the ruin of scientific objectivity'.[97]

In the later works, however, the debt to Saussure is apparent. Lacan accepts the Saussurean perspective on the arbitrariness of the relation between signifier and signified. This Sausserean claim, for Lacan, in *Function and Field of Speech and Language*[98] is important in so far as it discourages, he believes, a misleading, imaginary identification with 'the other'. We have seen how Lacan sees all self-consciousness, self-identity, as illusory. His suggestion is that a non-Saussurean conception of the relation between signifier and signified acts as a metaphor for an identification with the other, or with a perspective according to which one identifies with one's reflection in the mirror.

Once again we have a thinker associating non-structuralist, non-Saussurean views on meaning with a non-arbitrary connection between signifier and signified. In Lacan's case this link with the visual, specular imagery is clear-cut. He reverses the metaphorical connection between mirror symbolism and language. Instead of the mirror symbolism acting as a metaphor for meaning, things are the other way about. Yet he shares with other anti-realists the perspective on realism whereby signifiers picture/mirror their referents. As we have seen, this is a misleading characterisation of realism.

Furthermore, again like Derrida, Lacan accepts that one can study language independently of its referents. 'The signifier [he says] has its own laws, independent of the signified.'[99] In other words, Lacan accepts the Saussurean point that language is like chess; one can study its rules and its operations, independent of its function of referring to the real world. But, as we have seen, this is a misleading characterisation of language. Language, we saw, is not like chess.

The interpretation of signs, for Lacan as with Saussure, depends on their interconnection with all other signs 'in that structure each element assumes its precise function by being different from the others' and 'signification is realised only on the basis of a grasp of things in their totality.'[100] No act of reference can take place independent of language as a whole. Again, this is a view we have already subjected to criticism.

But it is surely partly this Saussurean perspective on language which leads Lacan to the view that: 'speech is moving towards nothing less than a transformation of the subject to whom it is addressed ...'[101] He gives his famous examples: the statement 'you are my wife' bestows that new reality on its addressee. The individual becomes wife by being addressed that way. Again, I would argue that this is a misleading anti-realist aspect of Lacan's thought. A person either is or is not a wife. She doesn't become one through being so labelled (except, in this case, in the special case of the wedding ceremony). Lacan is extending the consequence we noted earlier of Saussurean linguistics, whereby each new linguistic acquisition alters the language as a whole, to the relation between language and reality. Because, in the Lacanian system, the language – the speech patterns, the Saussurean *parole* – creates reality, it does so on each occasion the subject uses it.

A further aspect of Lacan's structuralism and his anti-realism occurs in his attitude towards the past. Analysis, according to him, is not a re-living of the past, but a 'reconstruction' of it: 'It is less a question of remembering than of re-writing history.'[102]

Analysis, therefore, is not concerned with discovering 'facts', about the life history of the patient. All one has to go on, after all, in analysis is: 'the patient's speech'.[103]

I accept that in the matter of the unconscious and of fantasy 'truth' may be a misleading epithet. Yet it is not just in this realm, as we have seen, that Lacan is an anti-realist. His anti-realism expresses itself in may facets of his thought.

One final area is that, for Lacan, the symbolic system determines individual subjectivity. There is no subjectivity outside language. There can be no thoughts independent of language. The analyst, Lacan says, must not uncover an 'imaginary intention' from 'the symbolic relation in which it is expressed'.[104] 'Nothing must be read into it (the symbolic expression) concerning the ego of the subject ...'[105] Now while it is true that thoughts – beliefs, intentions etc. – are formulated in language, we have already suggested that, as the realist argues, one can have some thoughts without being in possession of the word for that thought.

So Lacan, too, is an anti-realist.

Irigaray

Irigaray also is, in some voices, an anti-realist. She suggests that 'the feminine cannot signify itself in any proper meaning, proper name, or concept, not even that of women.'[106] She denies that she 'is making women the *subject* or the *object* of a theory'.[107] In other words, like Derrida and like Lacan, she denounces *reference*. The term 'woman' does not, according to her, gain any part of its meaning from referring to women. Its meaning, rather, like Saussure's terms, derives from its place in language – its place, specifically in two discourses: feminine language and 'phallocentric' discourse. As we have seen, feminine language can only be hinted at, in mimicry and metaphor. The mystic speaks it, and so does the hysteric. It is a language rich in revelations, but poor in devices enabling reasoning to take place. One might never arrive at a specification of the meaning of any term in this language, for, as we have seen, it is possible we can say nothing about it more than 'the incoherent babblings of a baby'. This language is in direct contrast with 'phallogocentric' discourse.

But these are anti-realist claims. Anti-realists, like Feyerabend, suggest that the 'discourse' of Einstein is incommensurable with that of Newton. The respective uses of the term 'mass' in the languages of the two are utterly different in meaning. The two men occupy different 'realities'. They live in different worlds. Now, as we have seen, Irigaray's 'feminine' language is incommensurable with the 'male' language of reason in analogous fashion. Men and women, as a consequence, live in different worlds, speak in ways that are incomprehensible to one another. The realist, as we have seen, views things differently. She does not take the partial variation in senses of terms like 'mass' in any two theories to indicate a difference in *reference*. Reference, and the world, remain constant in any alteration of theory. Thus had Irigaray been a realist she would not have spoken of developing different *languages* or occupying radically disparate realities. A realist Irigary would have recognised that there must be some commonality of sense between the language of the 'masculinist' and that of the feminist. The realist would say, moreover, that only if this is the case can one hope to bring about changes in *reality*. Sexism, she would contend, is a real phenomenon, existing in the real world, and is not confined to language. In her essay on Freud 'The Blind Spot of an Old Dream of Symmetry', in *Speculum*, the real Irigaray concurs with Freud (whom she has just quoted):

> One can only agree in passing that it is impossible exhaustively to represent what women might be, given that a certain economy of representation – inadequately perceived by psychoanalysis, at least in the 'scientific discourse' that it speaks – functions through a tribute to woman that is never paid or even assessed. The whole problematic of Being has been elaborated thanks to that loan. It is thus, in all exactitude, unrealisable to *describe the being* of woman.[108]

Woman is represented as 'other' in the language of phallocentrism. Therefore, according to Irigaray, one cannot (except in mystic discourse) describe her at all. But the realist would intervene here, and proclaim that even if it is true that woman is 'absent' from certain forms of representation, the term 'woman' is not 'absent' in language. Although the sense given to the term in the Freudian corpus Irigaray is examining may be such as to render her invisible *in Freudian theory*, or in Platonic theory (only some parts of it) she is *not* absent from language. Women and the feminine are not even absent from Freud's writings: Irigaray herself quotes a myriad of occurences of the terms. What is absent from Freud's discourses is a sense for the terms 'feminine' and 'woman' which valorises women positively, in the fashion Irigaray would like. The appropriate response to Freud, I would suggest, in realist vein, is not to renounce altogether 'the language of masculinism', but to retain the term 'woman' part of the sense of which is to refer to real women, and alter its meaning. As Mary Daly suggests, certain terms should be revalorised, from a feminist perspective (not a *feminine* one). This should not, now *contra* Daly, lead to the conclusion that there is a separate female *language*, rather it ought to lead one to think that some men have previously been using these terms *about women wrongly*. Really women are not as Freud characterises them. Part of the sense of the term 'woman', in Freudian theory, then, is wrong.

One aspect of Irigaray's anti-realism can be uncovered, therefore, by looking at her views on 'phallocentrism' in language. But Irigaray is also like Derrida and like Lacan, I believe, in her perspective on 'phallocentric' discourse. Like her predecessors, she associates the view that there is reference in language with its analogue in the theory of Cartesian self-certainty – the quasi Lockean view that words are direct symbols of mental experience. When she denounces the phallocentrism of the philosophical tradition, this is ultimately what she has in mind. Throughout her writings Irigaray associates masculinity with visual symbols, and particularly with the adopting of subject position in mirror symbolism. This occurs most starkly in her piece on Descartes, in *Speculum*, 'The Eye of a Man recently Dead', but we see it elsewhere. Female nature, in the tradition, she says, is characterised by lack, and a lack of something visible. When the Freudian or Lacanian little girl looks in the mirror, since the focus of her looking is supposed to be the penis, she sees nothing. Thus, when she looks there is nothing to see. Woman is what the masculine man is not: she becomes associated with qualities the masculine man either does not possess, or that he seeks to transcend: the womb, the earth, matter, receptacle, or in the Freudian case – nothing.

The metaphor, in language, that underlies all of this, is the Lockean one. Words 'mirror' or 'picture' things, in this perspective, as well as picturing or mirroring their senses. The relation between words, objects and concepts is analogous to the relation between the Cartesian self – the thinking self – and the cogito, the 'I think'. Irigaray: '... the specular make-up of discourse, that is, the self-reflecting (stratifiable) organization of the subject in that discourse'.[109] But this model of language, to reiterate once more, is not the only one there is for the 'phallocrat' (or for the feminist, what is more), who believes in realism and in reference in language.

So Irigaray, too, is an anti-realist.

Concluding Remarks

Contrary to Derrida's perspective, one can believe in reference, without being a strict 'logocentric' philosopher. Furthermore one could happily be a feminist critic of Freud without accepting that there are two languages. In other words, one does not have to believe, as all three thinkers appear to, that the meaning of the word 'table' is exhausted by its picking out the object in question, in order to uphold a referential element in linguistic terms. Similarly, referential theorists of meaning need not be strict adherents to the 'metaphysics-of-presence': they need not claim that referential terms are like the Cartesian 'I' in 'I think'; referential terms are not 'present-to-themselves' in the way that the 'I' is, for Descartes, in the act of thinking. There is, therefore, a position – indeed probably several – intermediate between the 'metaphysics-of-presence' and 'difference' or 'feminine' language. One does not have to deny *all* reference in denying the metaphysics-of-presence.

* * *

In this chapter, I have described some aspects of the thought of Derrida and Lacan, as background to Irigaray. I then argued that, although her work is indeed different from that of the 'radical' feminist writers criticised in the previous chapter, it does nonetheless suffer from its own problems. Finally, I have criticised the view of language on which, I claimed, all three thinkers rely.

6
Althusser and Ideology

In chapter 4 I argued that three conditions were jointly sufficient to explain women's oppression in a way that is integrated with the version of Marxism defined earlier in the book. These were: first, the biological fact of bearing children; second, the use of this biological data in class societies, and third, the way it is used and viewed in class societies – the 'ideological' factor. I will argue, in this chapter, that Althusser's perorations on ideology are of help to us in expanding on this third condition. But, I will suggest, we need to tread very carefully. My teasing out what is of use to us in Althusser's theory will be by no means a defense of the letter of Althusser's texts. Appealing to his own practice, I will draw on the spirit of some of his ideas on the subject.

Althusser and Ideology

One of Althusser's central claims in his article *Marxism and Humanism* is that humanism is an ideology, and not a science. There are two further main points he makes in this article. One is that ideology is a system of representations – images, myths etc., endowed with an historical existence and role in society, and distinct from science in that, in it, the practico – social function is more important than the theoretical. The other is that ideology is 'an organic part of every social totality'.[1]

In his essay *Ideological State Apparatuses*, written in part as a response to the events of May 1968, Althusser maintains the final thesis of the earlier article, but expands on the nature and function of ideology. He makes the point that every 'social formation' has to reproduce itself. He paraphrases Marx: 'every child knows that a social formation that did not reproduce the conditions of production at the same time as it produced, would not last a year.'[2] Every social formation, Althusser explains, must reproduce its productive forces and its relations of production. How does it do this? The reproduction of raw materials, instruments of production

122

and part of that of labour power occurs, as Marx describes it in *Capital*, in the labour process. The *material* means of reproduction of labour power – the provision of a wage – takes place there. But there is a further aspect of the reproduction of labour power. As well as the reproduction of the economic conditions necessary to maintain the workforce, there is also the reproduction of the worker's attitudes, her adherence to the 'rules' of correct behaviour etc., the reproduction of the appropriate level of skill in the worker. The latter will involve, for example, the association of certain types of task with masculinity and others with femininity.

Ideology functions in 'apparatuses', devices he calls Ideological State Apparatuses (ISAs). Examples he gives of such things are: the Church, the School, the Trade Union, the Family. ISAs, he says, are part of the 'private' domain. Althusser would argue, I think, that although the Trade Union is not, in most political theory, regarded as being part of the private domain, much of its functioning is somehow private.

Althusser argues that, in the mode of production characterised by serfdom, the dominant ISA was the Church. Religious, educational and cultural conformity, he believes, was largely ensured by it. Nowadays, he suggests, the 'Family–School couple' has replaced the role of the Church as the dominant ISA. In general, then, it is ideology that reproduces the individual as a particular kind of self.

Ideologies – religious, political etc., which he defines as 'systems of ideas which dominate the mind of a person or social group' – for Althusser represent 'the imaginary relationship of individuals to their real conditions of existence'.[3]

One of the foremost influences on the Althusser who wrote the ISAs article was Jacques Lacan. In Althusser's article *Freud and Lacan*, originally written, he informs us, to urge members of the PCF (French Communist Party) to recognise the science of psychoanalysis, Althusser askes us to re-read Freud. We must read Freud as we read Marx, Freud purged of biologism and psychologism. Freud, he says, like the early Marx, was forced to 'think' his discoveries in borrowed clothes, in the 'imported concepts' dominated by the sciences of thermodynamic physics, political economy and biology. Instead we must refer to Lacan's interpretation of Freud, for, according to Lacan, Freud founded a science, the science of a new object, the unconscious. A return to Freud is therefore a return to the mature Freud.

Althusser asks:

> What is the *object* of psycho-analysis? It is *what* analytical tech-
> nique deals with in the analytical practice of the cure, i.e. not the
> cure itself ... but the *effects*, prolonged into the surviving adult, of
> the extraordinary adventure which from birth to the liquidation
> of the Oedipal phase transforms a small animal conceived by a
> man and a woman into a small human child.[4]

And what is this Oedipal phase?:

> ... in the Oedipal phase the sexed child becomes a sexual human
> child (man or woman) by testing its imaginary fantasms against
> the symbolic, and if all 'goes well' finally becomes and accepts
> itself as what it is: a little boy or little girl among adults, with
> the rights of a child in this adult world, and, like all children with
> the full *right* to become one day 'like daddy' i.e. a masculine
> human being with a wife (and no longer only a mother), or 'like
> mummy' i.e. a feminine human being with a husband (and not
> just a father) – these things are only the destination of the long
> forced march towards human childhood.[5] ... all the material of
> this ultimate drama is provided by a previously formed
> language, which, in the Oedipal phase, is centred wholly around
> the signifier *phallus*.[6]

It appears that the influence of Lacan has to do, specifically, with
Althusser's perspective on the child's assumption of a gender.
Althusser appears to be buying, wholesale, the Lacanian re-reading
of Freud on the acquisition of gender identity.

I will argue that there are, in fact, two aspects to Althusser's appropriation of Lacan: one concerns the individual's taking on of
subjectivity – his or her acquisition of a sense of self-identity. The
other is more specifically to do with the conditions under which
boys and girls become *gendered* selves. I will argue that the letter of
Althusser's text is misleading on both accounts. Looking instead to
the spirit of his writings, and reading between the lines of his texts, I
will argue that we can uncover a true theory about the acquisition of
gender identity, and that this theory will provide us with the required filling out of the third necessary condition for the explanation
of women's oppression. I will look first, however, at Althusser's
appropriation of Lacanian theory on the acquisition of subjectivity
in general.

Althusser and Subjectivity

The classical account of subjectivity is given by René Descartes, in the sixteenth century. According to Descartes, I might be wrong about everything, therefore I must doubt everything. 'I must withold assent ... from what is not plainly certain.'[7] Descartes supposes he might be being deceived in everything he thinks. But, he says,

> let him deceive me as much as he likes, he shall never be able to cause me to be nothing, so long as I think I am something. So that after having thought carefully about it, and having scrupulously examined everything, one must then, in conclusion, take it as assured that the proposition I am, I exist, is necessarily true, every time I express it or conceive of it in my mind.[8]

Descartes, in other words, propounds what has been described as the 'reflection' theory of the self: the subject turns back on itself and grasps its identity with itself.

Now, a number of philosophers have criticised this theory. Fichte, for example, in his *Science of Knowledge*, argues that it is circular.[9] He claims that, instead of discovering the self in the act of reflection, as Descartes would have it, in fact, the self is presupposed. Only, Fichte argues, by presupposing that the subject of the act of reflection is himself, can Descartes claim that the self he comes to know is also himself.

We have seen, in the previous chapter, how Lacan, under the influence of Hegel, criticised this kind of argument. We saw that Lacan, following Hegel, argues that it is only through the recognition of the other's desire that the self gains a sense of self. In Lacan's view, the self gains an illusory sense of itself as a self through its seeing the 'other' – itself, in fact, reflected in a mirror.

For Althusser the mirror is used as a metaphor for those aspects of 'society' that the individual internalises. In the present context, the idea becomes the following: self-consciousness emerges through recognition of the 'desires' of society. The relation of the individual subject to society as a whole, for Althusser, is like Lacan's child's relation to its image in the mirror. Althusser says that 'the structure of all ideology, interpolating individuals as subjects ... is *speculary* i.e. a mirror structure...'[10] Society functions, for Althusser, like a huge subject that the individual sees reflected in the mirror: 'ideology', he says, 'interpolates individuals as subjects.' Thus ideology, for

Althusser, serves to mirror back to the subject, an illusory sense of itself as whole and unified. Ideology, he says, '"constitute(s)" concrete individuals as subjects'.[11] 'To take a highly "concrete" example, we all have friends who, when they knock on the door and ask, through the door, the question "Who's there?" answer (since "it's obvious") "It's me." And we recognize that "it is him", or "her".'[12]

Althusser clarifies that it is, indeed, self-consciousness about which he is talking, for, he says, '... you and I are always already subjects ...' 'But to recognize that we are ...'[13] In other words each of us is, in fact, already a subject, but we need to become conscious of this fact. In becoming self-conscious, we become self-conscious as a particular type of subject. We become self-conscious as a reflection of what someone or something wants us to be. He describes one example in detail: the 'subjections' of a subject to 'Christian religious ideology'.[14] 'The Christian religious ideology', he says '(says) I address myself to you, a human individual called Peter – in order to tell you that God exists and that you are answerable to him ...'[15]

Althusser goes on to claim that there can only be individual subjects on condition that there is another 'Unique, Absolute, Other Subject'.[16] An individual, he avers, becomes a subject (small 's') by being subjected to the Subject (capital 'S'). People become reflections of the Absolute Subject.

Just as, for Lacan, the individual as an (alienated) self-conscious being is a reflection of his/her image in the mirror, so, for Althusser, the individual is an (alienated) reflection of the Absolute Subject. Now, the one example he describes of this Absolute Subject is, as we have seen, God, who has often in the history of Western thought been so described. And the idea of the Christian self reflecting God's Will is quite common in Christianity. But Althusser also wants to use the idea of the Absolute Subject as a metaphor for a number of other 'ideological' aspects of the social world that the individual must internalise. So, instead of claiming, as some have done, that, for example, children internalise the rules of correct behaviour in school by being told them by their teachers, or through the 'material condition' of being a child in school, as others have done, Althusser says that children internalise this conduct by 'reflecting' the ideas of the teachers, the 'norms' of the school, etc. These latter become part of the 'Absolute Subject'. Althusser gives the following examples (apart from God): '(their) conscience, the priest, de Gaulle, the boss, the engineer'.[17]

Althusser wants to argue that the Lacanian metaphor is useful for explaining the individual's assimilation of 'ideological' behaviour.

He believes, as we have seen, that the reproduction of such conduct is essential if the relations of production of class societies are to be reproduced.

Reading the Althusserian metaphor loosely, an example of interpolation might be advertising. A good piece of advertising appears to appeal to an individual rather than the mass of consumers. Furthermore, it reflects back the fantasies of the individual, making things appear to her as though she herself were the author of the values projected. Thus, for example, an advert for women's make-up might appear to say: 'here you are; this is you as you could be if you wore this lip-stick.'

But, as Hirst has pointed out, there is a problem.[18] If we describe the human subject being 'interpolated' by ideology, then we are presupposing a 'pre-subject' individual already possessing the capacities of a subject.

There are a number of other difficulties with the account. First of all, some critics, for example Terry Eagleton in *Literary Theory*,[19] have argued that Althusser's picture is radically flawed: it appears to assume, he says, that the process of subjection to an ideology is total, unflawed, when, in fact, most people subject themselves to it only after a process of struggle.

I don't think that this criticism is a good one since, according to Lacan, the helpless infant's relation to his/her specular image is fraught with conflict. There is a constant dislocation, Lacan argues, between the infant's actual sense of him/herself as fragmented, disjointed, non-unitary, and the 'misrecognition' of himself/herself as unitary and whole – as a *Gestalt*. This dislocation, according to Lacan, unleashes an aggression both towards the child's own body and towards those of other children who, at this stage, are not perceived as being different from itself. Thus Lacan describes, in 'Aggressivity in Psychoanalysis' how, if another child is hurt, the first child will cry; and how, analogously, aggression towards other children may take the form of aggression towards oneself. Thus, to take Althusser's analogy, there is certainly conflict in the subject's relation to ideology: the individual both identifies with the School, the Family etc., as an imaginary extension of him/herself – and feels aggression towards parts of it. Perhaps, however, it is inappropriate to take the analogy too far.

Another problem, however, is that whilst it is plausible to talk about an individual becoming the reflection of another person, or of God, the metaphor does not function nearly so well for the relation between an individual and an institution, for example the trade union or the family. I think that, in fact, Althusser has another account of the process of internalisation of at least some aspects of the functioning of the family, and I will look at this below, but the explanation of an individual's subjection to trade union ideology is, I think, somewhat inadequate. Anyway, even in the case of the relation between two individuals – the individual 'subject' and the Absolute Subject, de Gaulle, for example, the Lacanian metaphor seems somewhat overplayed. One cannot *look* at de Gaulle quite in the way that the 18-month-old child looks in the mirror, and sees 'him/herself' reflected back. Few people would have had to have seen de Gaulle in order to accept his values. And, whilst Althusser doubtless does not intend the metaphor to be taken so literally, its value as a metaphor is somewhat attenuated if vision does not come into the process at some level.

Furthermore, there is a connection between Althusser's view here, and the perspective of his that was criticised in chapter 3. In that chapter, we argued against the Althusserian view that all human needs are brought into being in the production process. We were also critical of his implied view that individuals are merely 'supports' of relations of production. Now we see that not only are they 'supports' of relations of production, but they are also reflections of the Absolute Subject. But if they are only 'supports' or 'reflections' of relations and a subject that dominate(s) them, what   is the point of attempting to change these relations or these subjects?

Some critics, indeed, and E.P. Thompson's satire on Althusser[20] can be read this way, have made out that Althusser eliminates men and women altogether. In response, Althusser writes, in *Essays in Self Criticism*, that he did not intend his remarks to imply the non-existence of human beings. Instead, he says, he wanted: 'to render mechanisms intelligible by grasping them in their concept, and on that basis to render intelligible the concrete relations which cannot be grasped except via the "detour" of abstraction'.[21]

But, as Kate Soper argues

this seems to suggest that humanist and anti-humanist positions are compatible in the sense that the real nature of individuals is not in question: only 'abstractly' are they 'supports', concretely they are the rational and moral beings the humanist supposes them to be. Why then must they relate to themselves as 'träger' and not as 'making' history?[22]

Finally, there seems to be some confusion over what exactly Althusser is doing with the Lacanian metaphor. As we saw, Lacan certainly intends his original picture to function as part of the account of the individual's acquisition of (illusory) self-consciousness. And Althusser, we saw, appears to go along with Lacan in this respect. He seems to be arguing, against Lacan, however, that an individual can only gain (illusory) self-consciousness on condition that he or she becomes self-conscious *as a particular type of self* – as a Christian or a follower of de Gaulle etc. But this is surely not true. Even in class societies, where individuals are, in fact, particular types of self – communists, capitalists, etc. – this fact about them is independent of their possession of self-consciousness, illusory or not. The fact that a child, for example, has a sense of itself as a self is a separate matter from the question whether or not he or she is a Catholic or a Buddhist.

So this aspect of Althusser's theory of ideology seems to be flawed. But I will go on to argue that there is another side to his theory, so long as we read, after his own prescription, the 'spirit' of his writings rather than the letter, that is not only not flawed but can help us complete our broad explanation of women's oppression. This is his theory of the acquisition of gender identity.

It might be argued at this point that I have separated out two aspects of Althusser's theory which are indeed separable in metaphysical dualisms, but which Althusser deliberately and self-consciously conflates. Dualist theories, like that of Descartes, would split off the notion of self-consciousness from one's consciousness of oneself as a particular type of self, but this is precisely because they are dualistic theories. It is only because 'mental' and 'physical' life are separated in Descartes that one can do this. On the contrary, for Althusser, the process of becoming aware that one is a self is inseparably connected to the fact that one is a bodily self and therefore a gendered self.

I do not think that one needs to be a dualist to argue, as I have done, that one can be aware merely that one is a self, independently of the consciousness of oneself as gendered. All other aspects of the self would be, in the process, blanked out.

Althusser and Freud

In Althusser's article *Freud and Lacan* he appears to accept the Lacanian reading of the Freudian Oedipus complex. In the previous chapter, I criticised this account. I argued, amongst other things, that Lacan's use of the signifier 'phallus' seems to be arbitrary. Freud's original account, however, does not, I believe, suffer the same difficulties. I will suggest, therefore, that we take the 'spirit' rather than the letter of Althusser's text, and interpret him along much more classically Freudian lines. Locating Freudian theory inside the Althusserian Family ISA, I will argue, can provide us with an account of the way the biological data of childbearing is used and viewed in class societies. The biological data of childbearing is reflected in the gender roles of men and women. Thus we can use Althusserian theory to provide the third of our listed necessary conditions for explaining women's oppression. Althusser's 'family' ISA would become a Freudian family, with the gender roles of its protagonists reproduced in classically Freudian fashion.

An important caveat is necessary here, however. Freud has been criticised by feminists recently in all sorts of ways.

Before taking a detour, and outlining Freud's theory, therefore, I must mention some of the more important of these objections. I will argue that, although some of them do hold water, a version of his theory can, nonetheless, be accepted, that circumvents them.

The first fundamental objection is that gender identity – one's sense of oneself as masculine or feminine – does not exclusively involve a desire for the opposite sex, as Freud appeared to assume it did. Freud's account of the acquisition of gender identity (outlined below) therefore, would appear to be misconceived.

Secondly, many feminists have argued that gender identity is an ongoing process of conflict and interaction between aspects of a non-unified self.[23] It is said that although Freud sees the psyche as comprising a number of aspects, in conflict with one another, he doesn't really include gender identity in this process. He doesn't allow, therefore, as Ferguson puts it, paraphrasing Marx, that 'humans can change their own desires'.[24] The Women's Movement, Consciousness Raising groups etc., it is said, *contra* Freud, have changed women's senses of themselves as feminine.

Thirdly, as we have seen from the discussion of Irigaray in the previous chapter, Freud, it is said, by focussing on 'phallic' desire, fails to capture the diversity of women's sexual pleasures, not all of which are genital or focussed on orgasm.

Fourthly, the criticism has been made that the Freudian argument – that there are greater separation problems between mothers and daughters than between mothers and sons – is only true for white, middle-class families.[25]

Finally, it is said by many socialist-feminists that there are many sites of the reproduction of patriarchy besides that of the care of infants. Patriarchy is reproduced in schools, the work place, etc.

Apart from the final one, these criticisms of Freudian theory are, I believe, fundamental. However, a reading can be presented of his work, I will argue, which accommodates them. As for the final criticism, I would say this, in response. Even if it is true that 'patriarchy' is reproduced in many places, cross culturally, there must be some univocal fundamental explanation for the phenomenon. (Many socialist-feminists would agree with me not only that the phenomenon is well nigh universal but that it has certain universal features. Gayle Rubin, for example, once pinpointed the incest taboo, the asymmerical exchange of women by men, and compulsory heterosexuality as such features.)[26] Any equivocal explanation of the phenomenon risks not being an explanation at all. The advantage of Marx's theory of history is that it gives us a clear-cut causal explanation of class division. Within his overall theory, a great deal of variety in types of class society is possible; but that does not detract from the univocal theory. If the explanations for the reproduction of women's oppression are as many and as diverse as some feminists would have us believe then the 'theory' begins to look like those 'pseudo' scientific theories, which are confirmed by anything at all. Who is to rule out, for example, the restaurants, the cafés, the airports, as sites contributing to the explanation of the reproduction of women's oppression? It begins to look as though everything is part of the cause, and that it is therefore no cause at all. I would argue that although other aspects of society will play a contributory role in the reproduction of gender identity, there must be one area where it fundamentally takes place.

Some of the above criticisms of Freudian theory are now taken for granted by feminists. I believe it to be necessary therefore to take a detour, and describe classical Freudian theory, in order to clarify where his theory is working and where it is not. I will now describe classical Freudian theory, but with the following caveat: the Freudian family is read as an Althusserian ISA.

Freud and the Oedipus Complex

Freud, you will remember, believed that the nature of repressed wishes explains the generation of the seeds of masculinity and femininity. In fact, most of the evidence he offered was taken from boys and not from girls. Indeed, he sometimes apologises for 'dealing with one sex only'. But he did make some specific remarks about girls.

As is now well known, in his early writings Freud assumed, along with his contemporaries, that the sexes are not properly distinguished from one another until puberty. Later, however, he began to argue for their differentiation before this point. Central to his account is the Oedipus Complex. He says:

> I have found in my own case, too, falling in love with the mother and jealousy of the father, and I now regard it as a universal event of early childhood ... If that is so, we can understand the riveting power of Oedipus Rex, in spite of all the objections raised against its presupposition of destiny ... the Greek legend seizes on a compulsion ...[27]

The boy, in Freud's view, comes to love his mother and wants to get rid of his father, just as Oedipus did in Sophocles's legend. This 'Oedipus phase' in the life of the little boy is contemporaneous with the development in him of genital sexuality. Like its preceding non-genital stage, however, 'the phallic phase'[28] becomes submerged, and is succeeded by the latency period. The phallic period ends in typical fashion. When the boy's interest turns to his genitals, and this happens when the boy is approximately five years old, he makes it manifest by touching them frequently. He finds, however, that adults don't approve of this behaviour. Implicitly or explicitly, he feels threatened with the removal of the parts of him which have become so important. 'What brings about the destruction of the (boy) child's genital organization is this threat of castration.'[29] Freud argues that other things the boy has valued – his mother's breast, and his faeces, for example, have been taken away from him. Thus, the threat of castration becomes real for him. But the observation which really makes the boy believe in castration is the sight of the female genitals. Seeing a human being without a penis makes the threat of the disappearance of his own all the more real. Thus if the satisfaction of the child's love for his mother is to cost him his penis, and if, as he undoubtedly does, he wishes to retain his penis, he must renounce his love for his mother. Instead of desiring his mother, instead of wanting his mother as object, he comes to identify with his father: 'the authority of the father becomes part of his own Ego', and there forms the nucleus of the Super-Ego, which takes over the severity of the father and perpetuates his prohibition against incest. Thus the seeds of masculinity are sown in the little boy. If we incorporate the Althusserian image, here, the Family ISA through the medium of the little boy's identification with his father, has sown the seeds of a crucial component of ideological behaviour in capitalism – the seeds of masculinity.

Reading Freud through the eyes of the Althusserian ISA, we can say that the experience of identification, for the boy, will vary depending on the class, race and personality of the 'father', and on the way in which the particular family set-up is 'inserted' in the mode of production: on its interconnection with other ISAs etc. Thus, whereas according to some of his critics Freud eternalised Viennese middle class families,[30] this is not at all the case, if Freud's 'family' is read as an Althusserian ISA.

Freud originally took the formation of femininity to be the inverse of the process that takes place in the boy. But he came to recognise that things are more complicated for the girl. In dealing with the girl, he says, 'our material becomes far more obscure and full of gaps.'[31] One problem is that both sexes (given something that Freud took for granted, that is that *women* are primarily responsible for childcare), are originally cared for by their mothers. Therefore the mother (or female carer) will function, at first, for girls and for boys, both as the object with whom they identify, and as the one whom they desire. In other words, girls as well as boys, because of the structure of our parenting arrangements, will originally desire their mothers. Freud suggests that the clitoris, in the girl, when she reaches the phallic stage of her sexuality, will function like a penis. She perceives, however, upon making a comparison with boys, that she has, as Freud puts it, 'come off badly'. At first, Freud says, she believes that her penis will grow. Then she comes to think that she has already been castrated. Therefore, Freud believed, a powerful motive (the fear of castration) for the creation of the Super-Ego in the boy, is absent in the girl. Instead she comes to want her father to give her a baby: a substitute penis.

The Oedipus Complex, in the girl, is not resolved so dramatically as it is in the boy. In the girl, it is 'gradually given up' because the wish for her father to give her a baby is never fulfilled. Therefore she comes to identify with her mother and, this time, the seeds of 'femininity' are sown. The Althusserian family ISA, again, has fulfilled one of its functions.

Yet if the account offered for the boy is unsatisfactory, this one seems more so. Why should the girl abandon her desire for her father rather than go on hoping he will eventually give her a child? In the case of the boy, we are given a clear reason why he abandoned his desire for his mother: his fear of castration. But there is nothing parallel with the girl. Perhaps in recognition of this, in his later writings, Freud offered an alternative theory. According to this account, the pre-Oedipal phase is more important than the Oedipal one in the girl. The Oedipus complex has a long pre-history: the child discovers the genital zone as a source of pleasure, while still indulging in sensual sucking. At this point the girl notices the penis, and she becomes jealous of it. She 'recognizes it as superior' and develops 'penis envy'. She therefore gains a sense of her own inferiority. Originally, she, like the boy, is active and 'masculine'. Jealousy, Freud suggests, is more common in women than in men. As a consequence of the girl's penis envy, her bond with her mother is loosened; she both blames her for her own lack of a penis and deprecates her mother for not having one herself. She gives up her wish for a penis and puts the wish for a child in its place. With that in view, she comes to desire her father. Thus she becomes a 'little woman'. It is still the case, however, that the Oedipus complex is abandoned less easily in a woman than in a man.

In girls, the Oedipus Complex, according to Freud, is a 'secondary formation'. Whereas in boys, the castration complex destroys the Oedipus Complex, in girls the Oedipus Complex is made possible by the castration complex. 'Castration inhibits masculinity and encourages femininity.'[32]

Yet the above account must be qualified. First of all, Freud was at pains to argue that few men are 'purely' masculine and few women 'purely' feminine. In *A Child is Being Beaten* he describes masculinity and femininity as 'theoretical constructs of uncertain content'.[33] Indeed, as well as the Oedipus complex described above, he also admits that there is what he describes as a 'negative Oedipus complex' where the boy loves his father, and identifies with his mother. One of Freud's patients, the Rat Man, for instance, does this. Without the negative version, Freud's Oedipus complex, since it assumes that the child will become heterosexual, appears to contradict something to which he attaches great significance in the *Three Essays on Sexuality*, which is that both boys and girls are initially bisexual, and that heterosexuality has to be explained and not assumed. Secondly, Freud emphasised that the taking on of a sense of self is, in general, a fraught and difficult process – and is often not accomplished successfully. Finally, Freud believed that the concepts of masculinity and femininity are themselves imprecise. Thus, like the Lacanian self, the Freudian self is fragmented, split. We do not wholly identify with any one other figure. Thus, I would argue that Freud does not fall foul of the first two of the objections listed at the beginning of this chapter. Freud did not assume an 'innate' heterosexuality and his theory allows for conflicts within self-identity. Although, of course, he did not consider the phenomenon, his perspective can accommodate one's gender identity being altered by experiences like the Women's Movement.

Why, however, should we accept Freud's theory? On the face of it, it looks highly implausible, sexist and simplistic. It has been argued, for example, in the past that there is no likelihood of the child even being aware of the genital differences between its parents at the age of five or six, let alone its having the fears that Freud describes. Why should the boy be so afraid of castration?

Sexuality, as we have seen, is central to Freud's view of the acquisition of gender identity. The boy desires his mother, and this desire, for Freud, is at least partly of a sexual nature. The young boy is bound to have very powerful needs and feelings. The mother is usually the one to provide him with almost everything he wants and needs: she makes him comfortable by changing his nappy, she feeds him, she is there when he needs company, when he wants to be talked to, to be rocked or sung to. It would be odd if the young child did not have powerful loving feelings for her. And, the most likely description of much of the behaviour of very young children – the comfort they get from sucking (at anything), the pleasure and relaxation from rocking movements (both of which, in later life, come to be associated with our sexuality) is that it is, at least partly, sexual. Little boys hold on to their penises and do appear to derive pleasure from so doing. Little girls likewise engage in 'masturbatory' activities. So, the likelihood is that these two facts, that children have powerful feelings for their mothers and that they have sexual desires, will become connected. Little boys will have powerful sexual feelings for their mothers.

We know that in most cultures, powerful sexual feelings for one's mother are not allowed. The boy must come to recognise this, and the way this happens, Freud suggests, is that the boy becomes afraid of losing his penis, and then comes to identify with his father. Why should this be the way it happens? Many parents now notice a preoccupation among little boys and little girls with their respective genital differences at the age of five or six. They like to show off in front of others. The little boy's mother did not appreciate all that he had to offer. She did not appreciate his constantly shouting and crying for her for instance. She often failed to proffer her breast when he wanted it. Might he not come to think, then, that she'll take away his penis – his precious organ, the feature that appears to distinguish him from girls? So some of the power of his love for her subsides, and instead he comes to *identify* with his father: who also, like him, possesses a penis, and who, incidentally, also possesses his mother (but apparently legitimately).

So much for the boy. What about the girl? As I have already remarked, Freud's view of what happens here is less satisfactory than is the one he offers in the case of the boy. The girl both has powerful feelings for her mother which she must repress and she must come to identify herself with that very same figure. I think, in fact, in contrast to a number of recent accounts, that Freud's *earlier* version of how the girl becomes feminine is more plausible than the later account. It is true that the girl must come to recognize, just as the boy must, that her mother will not do everything she wants her to do. The mother will refuse to satisfy some of the girl's wishes; she can't always have the toy she wants, at precisely the moment she wants it. And these are constraints on what must be, in the girl, as in the boy, very powerful feelings for the mother. So is it not likely that she will look for some alternative outlet for her feelings? And the most obvious outlet is her father. What, she might ask, can he do for her? One major thing is to give her a baby. Freud's researches, documented in *On the Sexual Theories of Young Children*,[34] suggested that the gooseberry-bush theory of where children come from was much discredited in the minds of young children. His view was that young children do recognise that the arrival of babies is somehow connected with an event, whose description is unknown, that takes place between the man and the woman. Other writers, too, confirm that young children are well aware of where babies come from.

As with the boy, the powerful feelings the girl has for her mother will be partly of a sexual nature. Yet, like the boy's, these powerful sexual feelings for her mother are ruled out in almost all known cultures. So they must be repressed. But, unlike the boy, the girl doesn't have a visible sexual organ that she might lose. So her recognition of the cultural fact that powerful sexual feelings for one's mother are disallowed must be expressed differently. She cannot possess her mother, so that desire must be repressed. But she could be like her mother. Being like her in a way that is not significant for her as a sexual being like sharing eye colour or wearing the same clothes is no good, because the identification with her mother has got to replace her powerful sexual feelings. The most important and significant respect in which she is like her mother is that she, too, can have a baby. And who will give her the baby? Not her brother (if she has one) or her little boy friends, because they are not significant or powerful enough. The appropriate figure, given the realities of family life for many little girls, is her father. So she comes to want her father to give her a baby. This makes her like mother: a feminine being. Eventually, as this doesn't happen, she gives up the wish.

This account remains far less satisfactory than the one Freud has offered for the boy. It could be argued, however, that femininity is more problematic than masculinity because we live in a patriarchal culture. As Freud suggested, women are more subject to depression and neurosis than men, and the explanation he gave of this has to do with our social relations: girls, just as much as boys, have 'masculine' aims; they wish to be rational and independent. Because, however, these qualities are usually denied to women, they may turn these aims against themselves; the aims may be expressed as neurotic symptoms, or they may appear in the form of depression. For a typical example, take Freud's case study, *The Wolf Man*. The Wolf Man's sister was 'boyish and unmanageable' as a child. She then began a 'brilliant intellectual development'. According to Freud, she was more intelligent than most of her early admirers, but, in her early twenties, she began to be depressed; she eventually poisoned herself. This woman grew up at a time when intellectual activity was not acceptable in a woman. The acquisition of femininity has been, in the past, a more fraught, a more difficult process than the taking on of a masculine gender identity. Because of this, Freud argued, the woman has had less of a sense of self than the man.

Freud has provided an account, that fits with certain patterns, of a crucial state in the girl's passage towards femininity and the little boy's development of masculinity. He did, however, as has been mentioned, apparently take for granted that children are primarily cared for by their mothers. He also, as will become clear in what follows, took patriarchy, or the power of the male, for granted.

Women, in the Freudian picture, are characterised by what they lack; the penis. Emancipated women, he believed, were motivated by penis envy – they envied the man's possessing a penis. And they are just the extreme case: most women pass through the stage of penis envy *en route* to becoming 'normal' women. Sometimes women are completely absent from Freud's disquisitions: in *On the Sexual Theories of Children*, he admits that he is 'only dealing with boys', yet he does not head his work *On Sexual Theories of Boys*. 'Boy' for Freud, is sometimes taken to be equivalent to 'child': the girl is the deviant oddity.

The young child 'attributes to everyone, including females, the possession of a penis'.[35] The boy, when he sees the girl and realises that she doesn't have a penis, thinks 'hers is still small, it'll grow.' Thus, Freud's child believes that everyone has a penis. When he or she realises that they don't, that some are lacking this vital organ, the girl believes that she has been castrated. Instead of having a penis she wishes for a child, a substitute penis. Thus it appears that Freud attaches to the penis an inordinate amount of importance. All the major stages in the child's development revolve around it. What possible justification can there be for the penis's lordly role?

One argument (Freud's own) is that it is the leading erotogenic zone and chief auto-erotic sexual object. But of course, it is only such for the boy. It cannot, by definition, be such a thing for the girl. And the only explanation there can have been for extrapolating from the case of the boy to that of all children, is that Freud was tacitly assuming the male as the norm. There is, indeed, plenty of evidence that he was.

Perhaps, alternatively, the penis plays the role it does simply because it is visible. Boys value it and girls envy it because the former can see that they possess it, while the latter see that they don't; the girls just see that they lack it. (Janet Sayers seems to concur with this view of Freud, when she implies that the symbolic value of the phallus derives directly from the biologically given sexual character of the penis.[36]) But mere visibility is not, as I have already suggested, sufficient to give it such pride of place. Is it not likely that a rarer feature in a particular culture, such as the possession of red hair, would be more highly valued than a characteristic which half the population possessed? Why should the penis not be seen, instead of as a valued attributive, as useless excrescence?

Juliet Mitchell's reading of Freud in *Psychoanalysis and Feminism* is that it is not just looking and seeing the absence of a penis in the girl that produces the Oedipus complex in the boy; rather it is what is *symbolised* for him by this absence. Giving her own interpretation of Freud's phrase from his late work *Totem and Taboo*: 'ontogeny repeats phylogeny' (or 'individual development follows upon the development of the species') she argued that amongst all species, incest is desired, but again, in all cultures, it is forbidden. The Oedipus and castration complexes, for her, represent the individual's reflection of these facts about the species. Mitchell, then, reads the castration complex as the symbolic representation of the boy's coming to awareness that incest is prohibited. It is not so much the actual penis, then, for her, but a symbolic one – the Lacanian phallus – standing for power – whose loss is feared.

For Mitchell, then, the Oedipus complex represents the psychical implantation of the kinship structure and the incest taboo in the child. As Mitchell argues, Freud took it for granted that the penis has pride of place because he took male power for granted; he was dealing with sexuality, and the penis is the sexual organ of the male. Indeed, we may see how he assumed the power of the male if we look at his explanation, in *Totem and Taboo*,[37] of why the Oedipus complex is universal. He suggests, using anthropological evidence together with Darwin's theory of evolution, that there was once a 'primal horde', dominated by an all-powerful father who kept the women to himself, and who drove out or castrated any sons who dared to challenge him. The sons were driven to kill their father. But they both hated and loved him; thus they felt guilt about their act and symbolised him by a totem animal, which they would ritually consume. Freud was equivocal about whether this event really happened; he described it as a 'Just So' story. Nevertheless, he thought that the memory of it remained with us today, and that the Oedipus complex operated in its shadow.

However, this does not explain the Oedipus complex. The latter presupposes a powerful father, a father who is stronger than the son, and a father in relation to whom the girl comes to realise that she and her mother lack something. The boy wants to kill his father because he is powerful, he 'possesses' his mother. The Oedipus complex is not based simply upon the biological sex of the various parties involved. It is not just that the boy comes to recognise his difference from his mother and his sameness with his father. Rather, it is a complex based on the power of the father over his children and over his wife.

Freud assumes that the little girl comes to recognise a lack, an absence, in herself. She does not possess a penis. There is nothing about what she has: the theory is all about what she does not have. So, immediately, Freud is taking for granted that the father – the man – is a more powerful figure. In his second account (see p. 134) of the taking on of femininity, the girl does not have a gender identity of her own, different from that of the boy. Rather, she is characterised by what she does not have. What she lacks appears in relation to something the man possesses.

Indeed, it is the father, the grown man, who is powerful. The boy, at the moment, is not a proper man: he will become a man. While he is just a boy, he, like the girl, is relatively powerless. He is defined in relation to what he will become. Not what he is now, but what he will become is what matters.

Freud's 'Just So' story does not explain the Oedipus complex because just as the latter does, it presupposes this powerful father figure. For him the father figure is just a fact of life; a given that doesn't require explanation. Indeed, he admits as much: 'if psychoanalysis is phallocentric, that's because society is patrocentric.' (If psychoanalysis assumes the power of the phallus, that's because society is dominated by men.) Maybe he wasn't giving a prescription for a patriarchal society, but he was certainly taking its existence for granted.

So, Freud's account of the acquisition of gender identity rests on two assumptions. One is that women are the primary caretakers for children, and the other is the existence of patriarchy. Assuming these two things, he has explained the core of the acquisition of gender identity. It might be argued, however, that though the theory in fact assumes that children are cared for by their mothers, it need not rely on this. I think, in fact, that it requires only that children are raised by *women*, and that someone of the opposite sex is a significant figure for the boy. And he has this desire because his mother is the one primarily to confer love upon him.

Freud's Critics

One of Freud's critics in the 1920s and 1930s was Karen Horney, one of the earliest members of the Berlin Psychoanalytic Society. As a feminist, Horney sought to produce a psychoanalytical theory that was not phallocentric. She argued that both sexes equally envy each other. Whilst penis envy in the girl/woman is a straightforward matter (she envies the boy/man his ability to urinate standing up; and she envies him his scoptophillic drive – his ability to see his genitals), the boys's/man's envy of the girl/woman is more complex, and links both with admiration of the woman's ability to bear a child and with a fear of the female genitals. The boy, she argues, is afraid of his mother, because he desires her, and he is afraid that her large vagina will swallow up his small penis. The girl, according to Horney, takes her father as her first love object; her heterosexual desire for him is given from birth, and a sense of femininity is present in the girl from the first year of the child's life, deriving from her awareness of her vagina.[38]

Later on, after Horney had moved to the US, she argued that it is socio-cultural conditions that produce femininity in women: specifically, she came to believe, no woman need fall prey to masochistic tendencies unless she has neurotic needs to satisfy, through masochistic suffering.

One difficulty with Horney's writing is that the early material seems to assume an innate heterosexuality, while Freud had already argued that the clinical evidence suggested that heterosexual desire is acquired, and not inborn. Girls, Freud had argued, adopt the person who first cares for them – invariably the mother – as their first love object. As a consequence of Horney's belief in an innate heterosexuality, it appears as though she, in her early writings at least, took femininity to be a biological given. Certainly this is Janet Sayers's interpretation of her work: 'Horney implies that this acquiescence (to the hegemony of men's ideas in society) derives in large part from women's biology making them innately submissive to men.'[39] Yet, in *The Problem of Female Masochism*, Horney denies that masochism is inherent in their 'essential female nature'.[40] Instead, the girl seems to develop a sense of herself as feminine by means of a relation to herself – to her sex organs. But the difficulty here is that it is hard to see how she can come to see herself as feminine unless she has something against which to contrast herself.

Another problem in Horney's work, pointed out by Sayers, is that Horney, despite her feminism, seems to disallow women's resistance to their femininity: indeed, she treats such resistance as a sign of neurosis in women.

Given these problems, it is hard to see how we can regard the work of Karen Horney as an advance over that of Freud.

More recently, Jaqueline Rose and Toril Moi have argued (separately) that Freud's patriarchal assumptions render the theory itself suspect. They both criticise Freud in this kind of way, in a collection of articles concerning Freud's case history, *Dora, A Fragment of an Analysis.*[41]

'Dora' is Freud's writing up of the results of his analysis of a patient, Ida Bauer, who came to him in 1900 suffering from aphonia – a nervous cough. Dora's father, it emerged, was having an affair with a woman friend whom Freud labels Frau K. Herr and Frau K had been constant companions to the family, and to Dora, since early on in her childhood. Two events in Dora's life Freud picks out as significant. The first occurred when Dora was 14, when Herr K made a sexual advance toward her. She felt revulsion, and tore herself away from him. Dora also rejected Herr K a second time. Freud analysed

Dora's rejection of Herr K as both Oedipal and hysterical; Herr K, he said, represented her father, and her hysterical symptom – the cough – was the neurotic effect of her rejection of her own desire. Thus, her desire, according to Freud, was both hetrosexual – for Herr K and her father – and genital. The behaviour of the child of 14 was, according to Freud, already hysterical.

Rose argues, however, that the fact that Dora has a cough as an hysterical symptom is significant. It suggests that she unconsciously fantasises, through her symptom, an identification with her father. It suggests this, because the cough deepens her voice; it makes her appear more masculine. Rose goes on to argue that (as Freud later recognised) there is an element of lesbianism in all female sexuality that derives from the girl's pre-Oedipal attachment to her mother.

Rose suggests that Freud offers no adequate answer to the question: why does the girl relinquish this pre-Oedipal attachment to her mother? In his paper on *Femininity*, Freud claims that there are plenty of motives for the girl's wishing to disentangle herself from her mother: frustration of her oral desires to suck at the breast, for instance, and jealousy, ambivalence. The reason, in fact, Freud argues, that the child rejects her mother is because she (the mother) failed both to give her – the child – a baby (the substitute penis) and because the mother does not herself possess a penis. But, says Rose, if what characterises all these demands is the impossibility of their satisfaction, then the fact that there is another impossible demand ('the wish to get the longed-for penis') cannot strictly explain anything at all, other than the persistence of the demand itself – the question 'What does the little girl require of her mother?'[42] She goes on: 'What Freud's papers on femininity reveal, therefore, is nothing less than the emergence of the concept of desire as the *question* of sexual difference: how does the little girl become a woman, or does she?' The woman, Rose concludes, is neither subject nor object of desire: if she is object, whose object is she? Instead, we are left, says Rose, with 'the question of desire itself': there is no femininity; no feminine sexuality.

Rose is wrong, however, to argue that Freud's concept of a penis envy fails to explain the girl's renunciation of her mother. There is a difference between the various unsatisfied demands of her child. Though the child's demand to suck at the breast may not be satisfied each time, it is in principle possible for it to be. But it is in principle impossible for the mother to give the child a baby, so if the child does have this wish, she will eventually come to recognise that it is never going to be possible for the mother to satisfy it. Thus, if the child has the Freudian wish, then her coming to recognise that the mother cannot satisfy it might cause her to reject the mother.

Rose is surely reading too much into the Dora text; she concludes that, if Freud is proven wrong about the acquisition of masculinity and femininity, then the concepts have no application, and the girl does not become feminine. But, it is going too far to conclude that, just because Freud may be wrong about the way in which gender is acquired, the concepts of masculinity and femininity have no application.

Rose's argument does not work then; but there is an important point in her work, which is brought out by Toril Moi, in her article in the collection *Representations of Patriarchy*.[43] What is wrong with the Freudian analysis of Dora, Moi argues, is what is wrong with Freud himself: his failure to recognise his own patriarchal assumptions. Thus, in addition to the much documented phenomenon of transference – where the patient transfers onto the analyst some of the feelings he or she has for others – there is also countertransference – where the analyst transfers his or her unconscious emotions onto the patient. Moi argues that Freud unconsciously identified with Herr K, and he therefore is blind to any other influences at work in the text. Freud persistently refuses to consider feminine sexuality as anything other than passive. Furthermore, Dora poses a threat to Freud. She is a patient whose situation refuses to confirm his theories; she is a woman and she threatens his theories, and him. The root problem that's being pointed to, for Freud's theory of femininity, is the girl's pre-Oedipal attachment to her mother. Children of both sexes originally desire and identify with their mothers. When the boy realises that his desire for his mother will not be satisfied, it is relatively easy for him to identify with his father. The father, after all, is the most significant other figure and he is like the boy in one crucial respect. The girl's recognition that her desire for her mother will not be satisfied, however, is not so easily sorted out. One option available for her is to identify with the father: thus she becomes a man desiring a woman. Another is Freud's own solution: she desires her father in some way, and comes to identify with the mother. This makes sense of her obvious recognition that she is not, in the crucial respect, like her father.

I suggest that Freud's own solution *is* the appropriate one, if the girl is to become fully feminine, but that the other possibilities remain unconscious wishes for the girl. Thus, being feminine will be, as I have already said, more complex, more difficult, than being masculine. Lesbian sexuality in a woman will be more common, according to the theory, than homosexuality in a man.

More far-reaching criticisms of Freud have been made by people who are less sympathetic to him than are Rose and Moi. In *The Roots of Masculinity* Tom Ryan, an American psychotherapist, argues that findings from contemporary research challenge Freud in two major ways.[44] First, they dispute Freud's claim that gender is undifferentiated until the resolution of the Oedipus complex at about three to five years of age. 'Ordinary observation alone', Ryan says, 'can provide evidence that children, well before the age of three, know the difference between the sexes.'[45] Following Robert Stoller, Ryan claims that the child's 'core identity', which is the base from which masculinity and femininity are constructed, is established by 'imprinting' at around eighteen months. The parent will treat a boy differently from a girl, and this differential treatment is part of the imprinting process.

A second and most important point made by Ryan is that, contrary to Freud, masculinity and not femininity is the weaker and more problematic gender. From the fact that more men than women come to him with psychological problems about their gender identity, Ryan generalises to the conclusion that more men than women experience problems with their gender. Transsexualism, he says, where an individual feels that he or she is really a member of the opposite sex, is far more common in men than amongst women. Transvestism, the compulsive desire to dress as a person of the opposite sex, is exclusively practised by men. Moreover, Ryan claims, Freud's assumption (already criticised as patriarchal) that femininity is failed masculinity is biologically wrong: we all begin life as a female foetus.

The explanation for women being more secure in their gender, according to Ryan, relies, as does Freud's, on the fact that women are largely responsible for caring for children. The woman, Ryan argues, will have fewer problems with her gender because she simply has to continue to identify with her primary caretaker, whereas the little boy has to differentiate himself from his. The mother may not wish to give up the hold she has on her son, or she may experience him as an extension of herself, and thereby exclude any expression of autonomy or masculinity from him.

But, to take the first of Ryan's points, the child's knowing the difference between the sexes is not at all the same thing as its having a gender. And it is hard to see how something so complicated as it having a gender identity can be 'imprinted' on a child before it is three. There seem to be two sorts of difficulties. Having a gender presupposes seeing oneself as masculine or feminine, and it seems odd to suppose that one can see oneself any way without having had experience of one's own, not merely a piece of behaviour imprinted on one. As Hegel and Sartre, as well as Freud, argued, acquiring a sense of oneself as anything at all presupposes being able to differentiate oneself from one's environment. And having a sense of oneself as gendered would certainly require this. Being able to differentiate itself from its environment presupposes that the child has already acquired certain skills and abilities that cannot be 'imprinted' on it.

One problem with the idea Ryan takes from Stoller, therefore, is that imprinting seems to be the wrong sort of process for the acquisition of gender identity. But the other is that it is questionable whether or not a child has a sense of gender by the time it is three years old. Some studies show that children as young as two have substantial knowledge of the features associated with masculinity and femininity.[46] Other studies suggest that, at this age, children cannot classify anything at all, let alone people into boys and girls.[47]

The Oedipus complex and its resolution, with its focus on the desires of the child (and not on what is given the infant by its biology or by its surrounding culture) offers an explanation of the child's coming to awareness of itself as a self. It accounts for the child's coming to gain a sense of identity, and, as part of that, an awareness of itself as gendered. The child does indeed have a sense of self-identity before it is four: at 18 months most babies can differentiate themselves from their environments. But the Freudian account of the way that this happens seems less problematic than others. The child partly learns from the mother how to see itself. And what, in the child, is most likely to bring about this awareness? Surely as Freud and others argued, the frustration of desires. Because some desires the child has are not satisfied, it must cease to see itself as merged with the means of satisfaction of its desires: the mother. It must, therefore, come to see itself as separate, as a self. Later it will come to see itself as a gendered self.

Thus, the Freudian Oedipus complex still seems to provide a more satisfactory account of the acquisition of gender identity than any of the others that have been proposed.

What of Ryan's general claim that men experience more problems with their gender than women, and that this is because of the greater difficulties they are likely to experience in differentiating themselves from their mothers? First of all, Ryan generalises to the claim that more men than women experience problems with their gender from very limited evidence. The evidence he looks at is men who have come to him as a therapist, with problems of various kinds about their gender. But there are plenty of people who may experience difficulties with gender who do not find their way on to any psychotherapist's couch, let alone Tom Ryan's.

Yet another criticism of my account is this: it may be argued that my reading of Freud eliminates one of the features that is important in the acquisition of gender identity, particularly in the case of femininity. This is that the taking on of gender identity is a difficult, complex, conflict-ridden process, often not accomplished successfully. It is not, the implication is, something that can either be easily acquired or readily eliminated. Women (and men too, in a different way) are subject to contradictory pressures. All of these things suggest that a sense of self, and including a sense of oneself as gendered, is something that women have only in fragmented, disjointed ways. My account, it may be argued, makes it all too straightforward, too clear-cut a process.

However, my interpretation of the Freudian account can explain the deeprooted sense that men and women have of themselves as gendered; also, and paradoxically, it can explain how this very deep-rooted notion is also conflict ridden. My interpretation of Freud has focussed on the Oedipus complex, and its parallel in girls. The Oedipus complex explains the deep-rooted sense of gender. But there is also the boy's 'passive' feminine side, and the girl's corresponding 'active' personality; these sides of the person are not eliminated in my account, and, of course, they may reappear in the form of neurosis, anxieties, or even in the more straightforward form of conflicts over one's gender identity.

Althusser and Freud

Critics of Freud have claimed that his theory does not provide room for the removal of gender roles and therefore of women's oppression.[1] But the Althusserian reading of Freud can allow for the elimination of gender roles. If the 'family' apparatus into which the individual were inserted were non-patriarchal, and existed in a society whose relations of production were non-oppressive, then, although the individual would still be reproduced as a particular kind of self, this self need not be a *gendered* one. It would still be an ideological self in this sense: the individual would be reproduced as a particular kind of self partly through reflecting the values of others. It would never have Cartesian self-certainty.

It might be said, however, that I have still not dealt with the criticism, outlined earlier in the chapter, that Freud assumes the white, middle-class family as the norm. Some of his assumptions are untrue of Black and working class families.

Now, whether or not the particular point mentioned by Joseph and others is true of Freud himself, it is true that his theory assumes a particular type of family. I would argue that he takes for granted two general facts about families: one is that children are primarily cared for, at least in their earliest years, by women; and the other is that there is a 'father-figure' who is, by definition, less obviously present, but paradoxically is dominant, partly just by virtue of this relative absence. These two general facts are present in the description of aristocratic, craft and peasant families in the feudal period.[48] Even though the families were extended rather than nuclear, male dominance was probably greater than in later periods. Relations between parents and children were certainly more formal and hierarchical. Later on, in the Victorian period, in the UK, both middle- and working-class families – although they differed very much from one another – also possessed the above features. Working-class women, in Victorian Britain, worked – often very long hours – for wages, whilst middle-class women did not, but women nonetheless carried out the primary nurturing tasks.

The above two features are reproduced, indeed, in the majority of families today.

It is no longer true that most contemporary families, in the UK and the US, for instance, contain 'working' fathers and 'housewife' mothers. Large numbers of 'families' are headed by women; some families are made up of two gay men, parenting children, some of two or more lesbian women, and many more families have two working parents, male and female.

Some of these family forms are beginning to subvert the creation of classical Freudian masculinity and femininity, and are contributing to breaking down patriarchy. In the 1970s and 1980s the position of women has improved worldwide. Many British workplaces have Equal Opportunities policies and creche provision. In Europe and the US, women are no longer automatically judged 'bad' mothers if they work for a living. The Women's Movement internationally (and the 1985 International Conference on women, in Nairobi, revealed that feminism is indeed an international movement), and some of the changes in social life it set in train, including the impetus to organise one's sexual and childcare arrangements differently, must accept some of the credit for these changes. (Yet there are, in the US and in Europe, powerful forces opposing feminism – the American New Right, the British Thatcherite focus on the centrality of the symbolic 'nuclear' family etc. Additionally, the economic recession has made these 'alternative' family forms difficult to sustain.)

It is important to point out that whilst, on the one hand, some of these new family forms are creating centres of resistance to patriarchal norms, on the other, some of them contain some of the most oppressed members of social networks. One reason for this kind of contradiction, as Ann Ferguson has pointed out, is that, for example, the majority of female headed households are poor. Two out of three poor adults (in 1980s' US) were women[49]; women head half of all poor families, and over half the children in female-headed households are poor. Some of these women are forced to choose between a meagre allowance from an ex-husband who may threaten to beat her, and destitution. Additionally, media images promoting the dominant symbolic codes governing parenting and sexuality, favour the minority family norm of two heterosexual parents, and a small number of children. Moreover, schools, work and many social services assume as the norm the 'classical' nuclear family. Thus, it is hardly surprising that 'new' family forms both create centres of resistance to oppression and tend to reinforce it.

Thus, in all kinds of ways, the 'normal' family in Europe and the US today fits the Freudian pattern. Many non-European families today, too, lie in perhaps more extreme ways, within the purview of the Freudian perspective. Nawal el Saadawi[50] describes how her grandmother (a Muslim) was acclaimed as the paragon of virtuous womanhood, because the only time she went outdoors in her whole life was to venture from her father's house to her husband's on the day of her marriage. She was, indeed, 'present' for her children, and supremely under the control of the 'absent' father/husband.

The question might be raised, however, why I have continued to use the expression 'family', instead of, for example, some more general expression covering modes of parenting and childcare. Deleuze and Guattari[51] label these modes 'systems of desiring production' and Rubin has called them 'sex/gender systems'. Ferguson, recently, has coined the expression systems of 'sex/affective production'. She says:

My central theoretical claim is that there are historically various ways of organising, shaping and moulding the human desires connected to sexuality and love, and consequently to parenting and social bonding. It is in part through these systems that different forms of male dominance and other types of social domination are reproduced.

For my purposes, the term 'family' remains the most appropriate, I am attempting to offer a univocal theory of the reproduction of women's oppression, and the majority of 'sex/gender systems' throughout history, have been 'families' in the senses described. Although it is very important to point out that some 'families' today do not take that form, these unfortunately remain a minority.

Althusser's Family ISA can be seen as a Freudian family, then, as far as the reproduction of gender roles is concerned. How, though, on this reading of the 'family ISA' is it *ideological*? Is it ideological in Althusser's senses? I would argue that the answer to this question is in the affirmative.

The family ISA is in part ideological, in one of Althusser's senses, because it reproduces subjects – gendered subjects – who are fit for certain types of work in the capitalist mode of production. It therefore contributes to the reproduction of workers with appropriate levels of skill. That is not to say that the family ISA is purely 'functional' for capital, for the family is also the site of struggle. The production of gendered subjectivity will take on different forms depending on the context.

But the family ISA is ideological, additionally, because it produces subjects whose gendered consciousness is never whole, pure and non-fragmented. Thus, subjects never have full 'scientific' knowledge of themselves, because such self-knowledge is never possible. The production of gendered subjectivity is an ideological process in another Althusserian sense – ideology is eternal. Though family forms can, and will, alter, and specifically gendered subjectivity may cease to exist in some hypothetical cultures, 'ideological' subjectivity in the above sense will always be present.

According to Althusserian Freud, there is not one type of experience of masculinity and femininity. Men and women are formed as masculine and feminine selves by their position in the family. But this position is influenced by the way in which any particular family is incorporated in the mode of production overall, and by its interrelation with other ISAs. Thus, for example, a woman's race and class will influence her experience of gender.

On the Althusserian reading then, Freudian family forms are ideological and historical. They are part of historically determined modes of production. Further, the relation between 'Repressive State Apparatuses' and the Family ISA is relativised. Thus, the re-written Althusserian model allows for a phenomenon much remarked on by contemporary black feminists, namely that black women as mothers encounter the state in different ways, in Britain today, from white women. Immigration controls, in Britain, for example, have split up black families.[52] Many black feminists, however, concur with white feminists in their view that the family is one of the principle sites of women's oppression.[53]

Freudian Families: Ideological and Work Apparatuses

I would argue that these Freudian families, although they are ideological state apparatuses, are also part of the 'economy'. In chapter 3, I argued that 'sex' is a natural need. I suggested that although the 'drive' is natural, this does not entail that sexual desire is instinctual, as some of the nineteenth-century sexologists assumed. I further argued, in that chapter, that the point or purpose of production is the satisfaction of basic needs. Since sex – or the need for reproduction – is basic, at least for the species as a whole, then one type of production will be the production of human beings. The care and nurturance of children, therefore, is a type of work. If follows from this that families are part of the economy; that relations between their members count as relations of production, as a type of work relations.

Families are both part of the economy and part of the ideological superstructure. On the one hand, there is a causal relation between families, as part of the economy, and as part of the superstructure. On the other, the relation between the two is one of identity. How can this be? In my article *Marx's Materialism or the Materialist Conception of History*[54] I have argued a parallel point about Marx's general view on 'conscious existence' and 'consciousness'. I claimed there that these two phenomena are both identical with one another and related causally. I referred to Kripke's view that statements if identity, if true, are necessarily true, because they relate 'rigid designators' (terms which designate the same object in any world in which they designate at all). I said that if a statement relating 'consciousness' and 'conscious existence' were necessarily true, then, for Kripkean reasons, it is unlikely that there could be a causal relation between the items designated. (The causal relation between a particular cause and an effect is unlikely to hold in every possible world). But, I argued, we do not need to uphold the view that the statement in question is necessarily true, because the terms do not designate rigidly.

Parallel arguments apply in the present case. The connection between families both as part of the economy and of the ideological superstructure will function like the relation between 'conscious existence' and 'consciousness'. In the above mentioned article, I suggested that we look at an identity statement between 'the one working on the production line' and 'the one discussing wages with the manager' (as instances, respectively, of 'conscious existence' – 'producer of use values' and 'consciousness'). An appropriate statement, in the present case, would be 'the one looking after the children' and 'the one reading Mills and Boon romantic fiction'. Here, if the two descriptions are true of one and the same person, then the one looking after the children is identical with the one reading Mills and Boon. But the relation between 'the one looking ...' and 'the one reading ...' is not rigid. Thus the statement 'the one looking ... is identical with the one reading ...' is contingent, but it is contingent because it designates different 'time slices' of the same individual. The relation between the two 'time slices', however, is also causal: the woman who reads Mills and Boon is conditioned by her role as a mother and caretaker of children. Thus, there need be no contradiction in holding both that families are part of the economy and that they are 'in' the ideological superstructure.

Conclusion

I have argued in this chapter that Althusser's family ISA can be read as a Freudian family. I have defended classical Freudian theory against some classical and recent objections; and I have argued that other oft-remarked difficulties with Freudian theory disappear if the Freudian family is seen as an Althusserian ISA. In particular, we see how the acquisition of gender identity is not an eternal, a historical process, but it occurs at a particular point in the development of a mode of production. Thus my own 'integrated' account of women's oppression circumvents the difficulties we found with some of the other attempts to mesh Marxism and Feminism.

Notes

Chapter 1

1. L. Althusser and E. Balibar, *Reading Capital* (London: NLB, 1970).
2. Gregory Elliott, *Althusser, The Detour of Theory* (London: Verso, 1987), p. 62.
3. See J. Piaget, *Structuralism* (London, Henley and Boston: Routledge, 1971).
4. A.L. Kroeber, *Anthropology* (New York: 1948), quoted in C. Lévi-Strauss, *Structural Anthropology*, (New York, London: Basic Books 1963), p. 278.
5. M. Glucksmann, *Structuralist Analysis in Contemporary Social Thought, A Comparison of the theories of Claude Lévi-Strauss and Louis Althusser* (London, Boston and Henley: Routledge Kegan Paul 1974), p. 15.
6. Ibid., p. 15.
7. A. Schaff, *Structuralism and Marxism* (Oxford, New York, Toronto, Sydney, Paris, Frankfurt: Pergamon Press, 1978), p. 4.
8. Ibid., same page.
9. See for example R. Keat and J. Urry, *Social Theory as Science* (London, Henley and Boston: Routledge, 1975), p. 124; R. Bhaskar, *A Realist Philosophy of Science* (Leeds: Leeds Books, 1975), p. 24, and throughout the book and see C. Sumner, *Reading Ideologies: an investigation into the Marxist Theory of Ideology and Law* (London, New York, San Francisco: Academic Press, 1979).
10. C. Sumner, *Reading Ideologies: an investigation into the Marxist Theory of Ideology and Law* (London: Academic Press, 1979), p. 102.
11. Keat & Urry, *Social Theory as Science*, p. 124.
12. F. de Saussure: 'Course in General Linguistics', in R. & F. de George (eds) *The Structuralists from Marx to Lévi-Strauss* (New York: Anchor Books 1972), p. 67.
13. P. Geach and M. Black (eds) *Translations from the Philosophical Writings of Gottlob Frege* (Oxford: Blackwell, 1960), pp. 56–78.
14. Lévi-Strauss, *Structural Anthropology* (New York: Basic Books, 1963) p. 34.
15. Ibid., same page.
16. F. de Saussure, *Course in General Linguistics*, p. 9, quoted in S. Timpanaro, *On Materialism* (London: NLB, 1975), p. 143.

17. See R. Barthes, *Elements of Semiology* (London: Cape Editions, 1967), Chapter 1, Sect. 2.3, pp. 27–8.
18. Ibid., pp. 27–8.
19. See H.G. Gadamer, *Truth & Method* (London: Sheed & Ward, 1979).
20. See R. Barthes, *Elements of Semiology* (London: Cape Editions, 1967) pp. 26–9.
21. F. de Saussure, *Course in General Linguistics*, C. Bally & A. Sechehaye (eds), in collaboration with A. Riedlinger (New York, Toronto, London: McGraw-Hill Book Company, 1966), p. 16.
22. See N. Chomsky, 'Knowledge of Language' in *Minnesota Studies in the Philosophy of Science* (Minneapolis: University of Minnesota Press, 1975) and D. Davidson: *Meaning and Truth, Synthese*, 1967.
23. See e.g. L. Althusser, *For Marx* (Harmondsworth: Penguin, 1969), pp. 102–3, 202–4, and elsewhere.
24. Ibid., pp. 204–7, 209–11, 213–17.
25. Ibid., pp. 194–202.
26. See Glossary, ibid., under *Structure*.
27. Ibid., p. 202.
28. Ibid., p. 202.
29. Ibid., pp. 202–3.
30. Ibid., p. 203.
31. Ibid., p. 203.
32. Ibid., p. 203.
33. See T.M. Knox (trans.), *Hegel's Philosophy of Right* (London, Oxford, New York: OUP, 1980).
34. Ibid., p. 166.
35. Ibid., p. 167.
36. Ibid., same page.
37. Ibid., p. 196.
38. Althusser and Balibar, *Reading Capital*, p. 187.
39. See 'Spinoza to Oldenburg', in J. Wild (ed), *Spinoza Selections* (New York, Boston: Charles Scribner's Sons, 1930), p. 291.
40. See Spinoza, 'Ethics', in Wild (ed), ibid.
41. Ibid., 1930, p. 94.
42. Ibid., p. 94.
43. H.F. Hallet, 'Substance and its Modes', in M. Grene (ed) *Spinoza: A Collection of Critical Essays* (New York: Doubleday Anchor Press, 1973).
44. All of which are of subject predicate form, see A. Macintyre: 'Spinoza', in the *Encyclopaedia of Philosophy* (New York, London: Macmillan & the Free Press, 1967), p. 532.
45. Ibid., p. 532.
46. Althusser, *For Marx*, p. 196.
47. Ibid., p. 196.
48. P.F. Strawson, *Introduction to Logical Theory* (London: Methuen & Co. 1980), p. 175.
49. See for example ibid., pp. 231–3.

50. Althusser and Balibar, *Reading Capital*, p. 189.
51. Spinoza, 'Ethics', quoted in A. Naess: *Freedom, Emotion & Self-Subsistence* (Oslo: Universitäts Verloget, 1975).
52. See D. Hume, *A Treatise of Human Nature* (Oxford: Pergamon Press, 1968) Part III, Sects. II, III, IV and XIV.
53. Althusser and Balibar, *Reading Capital*, p. 188.
54. See Paul Patton, 'Althusser's Epistemology: the limits of the theory of theoretical practice', in *Radical Philosophy*, No. 19 (Spring 1978), for an account of the conflicting senses of the term 'production' in Althusser – one deriving from a Spinozist reading of him, and the other from a 'realist' reading.
55. See Althusser and Balibar, *Reading Capital*, pp. 191–2.
56. See H.F. Hallett, *Benedict de Spinoza: The Elements of his Philosophy* (London: The Athlone Press, 1957), p. 9.
57. Althusser and Balibar, *Reading Capital*, p. 34.
58. Ibid., p. 14.
59. Ibid., p. 14.
60. Ibid., p. 35.
61. Ibid., p. 18.
62. Ibid., p. 18.
63. See J. Derrida, *Writing and Difference* (London, Henley and Boston: Routledge, 1978), pp. 278–81.
64. Althusser and Balibar, *Reading Capital*, p. 16.
65. Ibid., pp. 16–17.
66. Ibid., p. 21.
67. Ibid., p. 21.
68. Ibid., p. 20.
69. Ibid., Althusser quoting Marx, p. 20.
70. Ibid., Althusser quoting Marx, p. 21.
71. Ibid., p. 22.
72. Ibid., p. 22.
73. Ibid., p. 22.
74. Ibid., p. 22.
75. Ibid., p. 23.
76. Ibid., pp. 24–5.
77. Callinicos, *Althusser's Marxism* (London: Pluto Press, 1975), pp. 34–5.
78. Ibid., p. 54.
79. Althusser, *For Marx*, p. 69.
80. Ben Brewster in Althusser, *For Marx*, pp. 252–3.
81. P. Patton, *Althusser's Epistemology*, p. 13.
82. See ibid., p. 13.
83. See S. Freud, *The Interpretation of Dreams* (New York: Avon Books, 1965).
84. Ibid., Sect. IV, (A) & (S).
85. Althusser and Balibar, *Reading Capital*, p. 30.
86. Ibid., p. 33.

87. Ibid., p. 29.
88. A. Schaff, *Structuralism and Marxism*, p. 40.
89. Ibid., Chapter 2.
90. See S. Timpanaro, *On Materialism* (London: NLB, 1975) pp. 171–2.

Chapter 2

1. See Althusser and Balibar, *Reading Capital*, p. 111, p. 119, pp. 138–306.
2. G.A. Cohen, *Marx's Theory of History, A Defence* (Oxford: OUP, 1978).
3. T. Benton, *The Rise & Fall of Structural Marxism* (London: Verso, 1984), p. 134.
4. Althusser and Balibar, *Reading Capital*, p. 111.
5. Ibid., p. 306.
6. Ibid., p. 119.
7. Ibid., p. 138.
8. Ibid., pp. 138–9.
9. Althusser, quoting Marx, ibid., p. 187.
10. Ibid., p. 188.
11. Ibid., p. 187.
12. L. Althusser, *Essays in Self Criticism* (London: NLB, 1976) S. Locke's Introduction, p. 14.
13. Editorial, *Theoretical Practice*, No .2 (April 1971), p. 3.
14. N. Poulantzas, *Political Power and Social Classes* (London: NLB and Sheed & Ward, 1973), p. 62.
15. Ibid., p. 63.
16. C. Johnson, 'Edward Thompson, Eugene Genovese, and Socialist Humanist History', in *History Workshop*, No. 6 (Autumn 1978), p. 80, 81.
17. J. Banaji, *Modes of Production in Materialist Conception of History, Capital and Class*, No. 3, p. 6 (1977).
18. See G. Cohen, *Marx's Theory of History, a defence* (Oxford: Clarendon Press, 1978), p. 29, and W. Shaw, *Marx's Theory of History* (Stanford: Stanford University Press, 1978) p. 5.
19. K. Marx, 'Preface to the Contribution to the Critique of Political Economy', in K. Marx and F. Engels, *Selected Works in One Volume* (London: Lawrence & Wishart, 1973).
20. G.V. Plekhanov, *Fundamental Problems of Marxism* (London: 1908), p. 52.
21. K. Marx, *Misère de la Philosophie* (Paris: Verlag, 1908), p. 122.
22. Marx to P.V. Annenkov, 28 December 1846, in Marx, Engels, *Selected Correspondence* (Moscow: Progress Publishers, 1975), p. 34.
23. K. Marx and F. Engels, *Selected Works*, Three Volumes (Moscow: Progress Publishers, 1969), p. 70.
24. Norman Geras, *Marx and Human Nature* (London: Verso, 1983).
25. K. Marx and F. Engels, *The Communist Manifesto* (Harmondsworth: Penguin, 1971), p. 85.

26. K. Marx, *Theories of Surplus Value*, Vol. 3, quoted in Shaw, *Marx's Theory of History*, p. 56.
27. K. Marx, *Grundrisse*, trans. M. Nicolaus (Harmondsworth: Penguin Books, 1973), p. 495.
28. Cohen, *Marx's Theory of History*, p. 136.
29. Ibid., p. 32.
30. Ibid., p. 33.
31. Ibid., same page.
32. Ibid., p. 34.
33. K. Marx, *Capital* Vol.1, trans. Ben Fowkes (Harmondsworth: Pelican & NLB, 1976), p. 132.
34. Ibid., p. 644.
35. K. Marx, *Theories of Surplus Value*, Part 1 (Moscow: Progress Publishers, 1969), p. 393.
36. K. Marx, *The German Ideology* quoted in R.W. Miller, 'Productive Forces and the Forces of Change: A Review of G.H. Cohen's Karl Marx's Theory of History: A Defence', *Philosophical Review* (January 1981), pp. 103–4.
37. Cohen, *Marx's Theory of History*, p. 94.
38. Cohen, quoting Marx, Cohen (1978), p. 99.
39. See R. W. Miller, 'Productive Forces & The Forces of Change; A Review of S. A. Cohen's, Karl Marx's Theory of History, A Defence', *Philosophical Review* (January, 1981), p. 105.
40. Ibid., p. 28.
41. Cohen, *Karl Marx's Theory of History*, p. 35.
42. Ibid., p. 216.
43. Ibid., Ch. 8.
44. See my article, 'Philosophical Materialism or the Materialist Conception of History', *Radical Philosophy*, No. 23 (1979).
45. K. Marx, *The Poverty of Philosophy, Selected Works*, Vol. 1 (London: Lawrence & Wishart, 1968) pp. 518–9.
46. Shaw, *Marx's Theory of History*, p. 63.
47. S. Sayers, 'Forces of Production & Relations of Production in Socialist Society', *Radical Philosophy*, No. 24 (Spring 1980).
48. See S. Hook, *Towards an Understanding of Karl Marx* (London: Gollancz, 1933), pp. 88–9.
49. L. Althusser, *Essays in Self Criticism* (London: NLB, 1976), p. 89.
50. G. Elliot, *Althusser: The Detour of Theory*, p. 148, including quote from L. Althusser, *For Marx*, p. 104.
51. Ibid., p. 148.
52. L. Althusser, *For Marx*, p. 99.
53. K. Marx and F. Engels, *Basic Writings on Politics & Economics* (Harmondsworth: Penguin, 1969).
54. See Miller, *Productive Forces and the Forces of Change*, p. 101.
55. Ibid., pp. 99, 100.
56. See Marx, *Capital*, Vol. 1, trans Ben Fowkes (Harmondsworth: London,

Penguin and NLB, 1976) pp. 555–7.

57. Ibid., p. 411.
58. Ibid., p. 439.
59. Miller, *Productive Forces and the Forces of Change*, p. 103.
60. Marx, *Capital*, p. 439.
61. Ibid., p. 441.
62. Ibid., pp. 878–9.
63. R. Hilton (ed), *The Transition from Feudalism to Capitalism* (London: NLB, 1976), p. 111.
64. Ibid., same page.
65. E. Hobsbawm, in R. Hilton (ed) *The Transition from Feudalism to Capitalism* (Harmondsworth: Penguin, 1973), pp. 161–2.
66. Marx, *Grundrisse* (Harmondsworth, Penguin, 1973) p. 182.
67. See Cohen, *Karl Marx's Theory of History*.
68. P. Corrigan et al, *Socialist Construction & Marxist Theory* (London: Macmillan, 1978).
69. Marx to Otechestvenniye Zapiski, Nov. 1877, in Marx, Engels, *Selected Correspondence* (Moscow: Progress Publishers, 1975) p. 292.
70. Ibid., p. 293.
71. Marx to Vera Ivanovna Zasulich, 2 March 1975, p. 319.
72. Ibid., same page.
73. See K. Marx and F. Engels, Werke, Vol. XVIII (Institut fuer Marxismus – Leninismus beim ZK der SED, Berlin, 1964) pp. 556–7.
74. K. Marx, *Werke*, Vol. XVIII (1964), p. 668.
75. Elsewhere, Engels goes right away from this view, and suggests that '...the Russians are approaching their 1789. The revolution *must* break out there within a given time; it *may* break out any day.' (F. Engels to Vera Ivanovna Zasulich in Geneva, London, April, 1985, in Marx & Engels, *Selected Correspondence*).
76. Miller, *Productive Forces and the Forces of Change*, p. 93.
77. K. Marx, *Class Struggles in France* (London: Lawrence & Wishart, 1942) quote from F. Engels' Introduction, p. 16.
78. Ibid., p. 44.
79. Ibid., p. 56.

Chapter 3

1. Michael Ryan, *Marxism and Deconstruction* (Baltimore: Johns Hopkins, University Press, 1982) p. 56.
2. See Norman Geras, *Marx and Human Nature* (London: Verso, 1983).
3. See Althusser and Balibar, *Reading Capital*, pp. 166–70.
4. Ibid., p. 174.
5. Ibid., pp. 167–71.
6. Ibid., p. 166.
7. Kate Soper, in *The Needs of Marxism*, seems to accept a version of

Althusser's argument. She says: 'Instead of charting human development on the basis of a given human nature with its set of human defining needs he [Marx] historicises needs – and thus to the extent that human nature plays a part in his analysis, it itself is conceived as historical development, not as essence but as the sum of social relations at a given point' (Soper, 'The Needs of Marxism', *Radical Philosophy* (1977), p. 39). But this assumes that there is no separable biological nature and that what is historical must be 'the sum of social relations'. I do not see why either of these assumptions should be correct. Elsewhere (see K. Soper, 'On Materialism', *Radical Philosophy*, No. 15 (1976)) she does not make these assumptions.

8. Althusser and Balibar, *Reading Capital*, p. 166.
9. Ibid., p. 166.
10. Ibid., p. 166.
11. K. Marx, *Introduction to the Grundrisse*, quoted in Althusser and Balibar, *Reading Capital*, p. 167.
12. In my view, and I consider this also be Marx's, there is no difference between a 'socialist' and a 'communist' mode of production. See the *Economic and Philosophical Manuscripts*, the *Holy Family*, and the *Poverty of Philosophy* for interchangeable use of the words 'socialism' and 'communism'. In the *Critique of the Gotha Programme*, Marx says: 'Communist society ... when it has just emerged after prolonged birth pangs from capitalist society' (Marx, *Selected Works in One Volume* (London: Lawrence & Wishart, 1968), p. 324). And Engels tells us, in the Preface to the English Edition of the Communist Manifesto that 'though [the Manifesto] is the most international production of all *socialist* literature' (my emphasis) they could not have called it a 'socialist' manifesto because 'By Socialists, in 1847, were understood ... the adherents of the various Utopian systems ... and the most multifarious social quacks ...' (p. 62 Penguin 1927 edition, Preface to the English edition of 1888). For a very useful discussion of the concept 'mode of production' see G.A. Cohen, *Karl Marx's Theory of History, A Defence* (Oxford: Clarendon Press, 1978) pp. 79-87.
13. K. Marx, *Economic and Philosophical Manuscripts* (London: Lawrence and Wishart, 1973), p. 147.
14. Kate Soper, *On Human Needs* (Brighton: Harvester Press, 1981), p. 11.
15. D. Miller, *Social Justice* (Oxford: Clarendon Press, 1976), p. 127.
16. K. Marx, *Grundrisse*, p. 528.
17. Ibid., p. 528.
18. Ibid., p. 112.
19. See, for one such argument, E. Brandon: 'Reason not the Needs', in *Education for Development*, 1980.
20. B. Barry, *Political Argument* (New Jersey Humanities Press, Atlantic Highlands, 1976).
21. It might be said that there is an equivocation here; that, really, in the second case the need is for help with the washing. But I see no reason

why the claim has to be read this way. The housewife may not have considered other ways of getting the wash done – she may not have known about them; and others may fail to recognise alternative ways of satisfying her need.

22. See Rousseau and S. Ellenburg, *Discourse on Inequality*, quoted in *Rousseau's Political Philosophy, an interpretation from within* (New York: Cornell University Press, 1976), pp. 65–6.
23. I am indebted to Fred Feldman for this suggestion.
24. This example was put to me by a graduate student at the University of Waterloo, Ontario.
25. S.I. Benn and R.S. Peters, *Social Principles and the Democratic State* (Harmondsworth: Allen & Unwin, 1959).
26. K. Marx, *Selected Works in One Volume* (London: Lawrence & Wishart, 1971), p. 197.
27. D. Braybrooke, 'Let Needs Diminish that Preferences may Prosper', in *Studies in Moral Philosophy*, ed. N. Rescher (Oxford: Blackwell, 1968), p. 90.
28. Ibid., pp. 97–8.
29. V.N. Vološinov (trans. R. Titunik), *Freudianism: A Marxist Critique* (New York, Academic Press, 1976), p. 15.
30. Ibid., p. 10.
31. See S. Timpanaro, *On Materialism* (London: NLB, 1975), p. 10.
32. Ibid., same page.
33. Ibid., same page.
34. Ibid., p. 13.
35. Ibid., p. 13.
36. K. Marx, *The German Ideology* (London: Lawrence & Wishart, 1965), p. 39.
37. K. Marx, *Selected Works in One Volume*, p. 315.
38. See Ted Benton, 'Speciesism, Marx on Humans and Animals', *Radical Philosophy*, No. 50 (Autumn 1988) and Mary Midgley, *Beast and Man: The Roots of Human Nature* (Brighton: Harvester, 1980).

Chapter 4

1. Heidi Hartmann, 'The Unhappy Marriage of Marxism and Feminism, towards a More Progressive Union', *Capital and Class*, No. 8 (1979) and see also, Mark Cousins, 'Material Arguments and Feminism', *m/f*, No. 2 (1978).
2. Anne Phillips, 'Marxism and Feminism', in *Revolutionary Socialism*, No. 6 (Winter 1980).
3. F. Engels, 'The Origin of the Family, Private Property and the State', in K. Marx, *Selected Works in One Volume* (London: Lawrence and Wishart, 1968), p. 495.

4. Engels, *The Origin of the Family*, p. 499.
5. Ibid., p. 496.
6. Ibid., p. 499.
7. For one such study, see Anna Pollert, *Girls, Wives, Factory Lives* (London: Pluto Press, 1981).
8. Ibid., p. 499.
9. See Aristotle, quoted in J. Lloyd, 'The Man of Reason', in *Metaphilosophy* (1979).
10. Ibid., p. 19.
11. Christine Delphy, *The Main Enemy* (London: WRRC, 1977).
12. Ibid., pp. 15–16.
13. Valerie Amos and P. Parma, 'Challenging Imperial Feminism', *Feminist Review*, No. 17 (1984).
14. Shulamith Firestone, *The Dialectic of Sex: the case for Feminist Revolution* (London: Paladin, 1971), p. 15.
15. Wally Secombe, 'The Housewife and her labour under Capitalism', *New Left Review*, No. 1 83 (1978) and Jean Gardener, 'Women's Domestic Labour', NLR, No. 89 (1975).
16. See Betty Friedan, *The Feminine Mystique* (New York: Norton, 1963).
17. See Margaret Coulson, Branka Megas and Hilary Wainwright, 'The Housewife and her Labour under Capitalism, a Critique', *NLR*, No. 89 (1975).
18. See, for example, Angela Miles, 'Economism and Feminism, Hidden in the Household: A comment on the Domestic Labour debate', *Studies in Political Economy*, No. 11 (Summer, 1983).
19. Heidi Hartmann, 'The Unhappy Marriage of Marxism and Feminism'.
20. See, for examply, Michelle Barrett, *Women's Oppression Today* (London: Verso, 1980); J. Humphries, 'Class Struggle and the persistence of the working class family', *Cambridge Journal of Economics*, Vol. 1 No. 3 (Sept.); and L. Vogel, *Marxism and the Oppression of Women; Toward a Unitary Theory* (New Brunswick: New Jersey, Rutgers University, 1983).
21. Michelle Barrett, *Women's Oppression Today, Problems in Marxist Feminist Analysis* (London: Verso, 1980).
22. Pat Armstrong and Hugh Armstrong, 'Beyond Sexless class and Classless sex', in (eds) Roberta Hamilton and Michelle Barrett, *The Politics of Diversity* (London: Verso, 1987).
23. Ibid., p. 225.
24. Ibid., p. 229.
25. Ibid., p. 229.
26. See Anne Oakley, *Sex, Gender and Society* (London: Maurice, Temple Smith Ltd., 1972).
27. Maureen McIntosh, 'Gender and Economics: The Sexual Division of Labour and the Subordination of Women', in *Of Marriage and the Market* (London: CSE Books, 1981), p. 12.
28. Ibid., p. 11.

Chapter 5

1. See Janet Sayers, *Biological Politics* (London: Tavistock, 1982), p. 148; Lynne Segal, *Is the Future Female* (London: Virago, 1987), p. 133; Cora Kaplan, 'Pandora's Box; Subjectivity and Sexuality in Socialist-Feminist Criticism', in (eds) Gay Green and Coppelia Kahn, *Making a Difference, Feminist Literary Criticism* (London: Methuen, 1985), p. 152 and Toril Moi, *Sexual/Textual Politics* (London: Methuen, 1985), p. 139 and p. 148. The latter is a more sophisticated account of Irigaray, but she is still labelled 'essentialist'.
2. See, for example, Claire Duchen, 'Women's Difference', in *French Connections, Voices from the Women's Movement in France*, translated and edited by Claire Duchen (London: Hutchinson, 1987), p. 55.
3. See, for example, Michelle Barrett, 'The Concept of Difference', *Feminist Review*, No. 26, (Summer 1987); Ann Rosalind Jones, 'French Theories of the Feminine', in *Making a Difference, Feminist Literary Criticism*, and Jane Gallop, *Feminism and Psychoanalysis* (London: Macmillan, 1982).
4. Luce Irigaray, *Speculum, of the Other Woman* (New York: Cornell University Press, 1985).
5. Luce Irigaray, *This Sex which is Not One* (New York: Cornell University Press, 1985).
6. Irigaray, *This Sex*, pp. 155–6.
7. J. Gallop, *Feminism and Psychoanalysis*, p. 74.
8. Irigaray, *This Sex*, p. 162.
9. Toril Moi, *Sexual/Textual Politics*, p. 138.
10. Irigarary, *This Sex*, p. 74.
11. Jacques Derrida, *Of Grammatology* (Baltimore and London: John Hopkins University Press, 1976).
12. Ibid., p. 162.
13. See, for example, Newton Carver, *Journal of Philosophy* (November 1977).
14. See Jacques Derrida, 'Limited Inc.', *Glyph*, 2 (1977), pp. 162–254.
15. Jean Jacques Rousseau, *Essai sur l'origine des langues* (Bordeaux: Bucros, 1968), Chapter 2.
16. Jean Jacques Rousseau, *Discourse on Inequality* (London: Everyman, 1966).
17. Jacques Derrida, *Of Grammatology*, p. 173.
18. Jacques Derrida, ibid., p. 173.
19. Jacques Derrida, ibid., p. 182.
20. Jean Jacques Rousseau, *The Confessions*, Book VIII (London, Penguin, 1984).
21. Jean Jacques Rousseau, ibid., p. 155.
22. Jacques Derrida, *Of Grammatology*, p. 159.

23. Jonathan Culler, *On Deconstruction, Theory and Criticism after Structuralism* (London: Routledge, 1987), p. 104.

24. Jean Jacques Rousseau, quoted in Jacques Derrida, *Of Grammatology*, p. 208.

25. Jean Jacques Rousseau, *Émile*, quoted in Jacques Derrida, *Of Grammatology*, p. 211.

26. Jacques Lacan, *Écrits: A Selection* (London: Tavistock, 1977), p. 114.

27. Sigmund Freud, 'Project for a Scientific Discovery', in *The Origin of Psychoanalysis*, eds. M. Bonaparte, A. Freud and E. Kris (London: Hogarth, 1954), (1985).

28. Sigmund Freud, *On Narcissism, An Introduction*, SE XIV, pp. 67–102.

29. Sigmund Freud, ibid., p. 77.

30. Sigmund Freud, *The Ego and the Id*, SE XIX, 1923, p. 26.

31. Jacques Lacan, 'The Mirror Stage as formative of the I as revealed in psychoanalytic experience' (1949), in *Écrits: A Selection* (London: Tavistock, 1977).

32. J.W.F. Hegel, *The Phenomenology of Spirit*, trans A.V. Miller (Oxford: OUP, 1979).

33. Jacques Lacan, *The Mirror Stage*, p. 2.

34. Jacques Lacan, *The Mirror Stage*, p. 2.

35. Jacques Lacan, *Discours de Rome, Le Seminaire Livre III, Les Psychoses* (Paris: 1981), Chapter 14.

36. Jacques Lacan, *Écrits, A Selection*, p. 126.

37. Peter Dews, *Logics of Disintegration, Post Structuralist Thought and the Claim of Critical Theory* (London: Verso, 1987), p. 84.

38. Peter Dews, *Logics of Disintegration*, p. 84.

39. Jacques Lacan, 'La relation d'objet et les structure freudiennes – compte rendu du 4th seminar', *Bulletin de Psychologie*, Vol. XI (1957) trans by Peter Dews in Logics of Disintegration, p. 85.

40. Jacques Derrida, *Positions* (Chicago: University of Chicago Press, 1981), p. 41.

41. Luce Irigaray, *This Sex which is not One*, p. 155.

42. Ibid., pp. 155–6.

43. Ibid., p. 74.

44. Ibid., p. 68.

45. Ibid., p. 68.

46. Toril Moi, *Sexual/Textual Politics*, p. 130.

47. Ibid., p. 130.

48. Andrea Nye, *Feminist Theory and the Philosophies of Man* (London: Croom Helm, 1988), p. 151.

49. Luce Irigaray, *Speculum*, p. 183.

50. Ibid., p. 183.

51. Ibid., p. 191.

52. Ibid., p. 191.

53. Ibid., p. 191.

54. Ibid., p. 192.

55. Ibid., p. 192.
56. Ibid., p. 193.
57. Jacques Lacan, 'The Mirror Stage', in *Écrits, A Selection*, p. 12.
58. Monique Plaza, 'Phallomorphic Power and the Psychology of Women', *Ideology and Consciousness* (Autumn 1978), pp. 4–36.
59. Hélène Cixous, 'Le Rire de la Meduse', *L'Arc*, 61, trans. 'The Laugh of the Medusa', in Marks, Elaine and Coutivron, Isabelle de, *New French Feminisms* (Brighton: Harvester, 1980), p. 253.
60. Luce Irigaray, *This Sex*, p. 25.
61. Ibid., pp. 25–6.
62. Ibid., p. 33.
63. Ibid., p. 33.
64. Andrea Nye, *Feminist Theory*, p. 152.
65. Maurice Merleau Ponty, *The Phenomenology of Perception* (London: RKP, 1962), p. 354.
66. Shoshana Felman, 'The Critical Phallacy', *Diacritics* (Winter 1975), pp. 2–10, quoted in Toril Moi, *Sexual/Textual Politics*, p. 138.
67.. Ibid., p. 147.
68. Ibid., p. 147.
69. J. Koethe quoting Hilary Putnam, 'Putnam's Argument against Realism', *Philosophical Review*, (1979), p. 92.
70. R. Bhaskar, *A Realist Theory of Science* (Leeds: Leeds Books, 1975), p. 22.
71. G. Bachelard, *Le Nouvel Esprit Scientifique* (Paris: Presses Universitaires de France, 1934), pp. 12–13.
72. Koethe, again quoting Putnam, in Koethe, *Putnam's Argument against Realism*, p. 93.
73. Ibid., p. 94.
74. Colin McGinn, 'A Note on the Essence of Natural Kinds', *Analysis*, 35 (1974–5).
75. D. Davidson and G. Harman (eds), *Semantics of Natural Languages* (Dortrecht: Reidel, 1972), p. 320.
76. Ibid., p. 321.
77. J. Locke, *Essay Concerning Human Understanding* (London: The Fontana Library, 1964), Book III, IX, Section 18, p. 271.
78. Ibid., Book IV, II, 2-7, pp. 326–8.
79. Locke, *Essay*, Book IV, III, 25, pp. 326–8.
80. Hilary Putnam, *Mind, Language and Reality* (Cambridge: CUP, 1975), p. 231.
81. Paul Feyerabend, 'Explanation, Reduction and Empiricism', in *Minnesota Studies in the Philosophy of Science* (Minneapolis: University of Minnesota Press, 1962), pp. 80–1.
82. Paul Feyerabend, 'How to be a Good Empiricist – a Plea for Tolerance in Mallers Epistemological', in B.A. Brody (ed.) *Readings in the Philosophy of Science* (New Jersey: Prentice Hall, 1970), p. 326.
83. F. de Saussure, *Course in General Linguistics*.
84. Ibid., p. 88.

85. J. Derrida, *Of Grammatology*, p. 44.
86. Ibid., p. 35.
87. Ibid., p. 35.
88. Ibid., p. 31.
89. Ibid., p. 31.
90. Ibid., p. 11.
91. J. Derrida, *Writing and Difference*.
92. Ibid., p. 280.
93. Ibid., p. 280.
94. J. Derrida, *Glas* (Paris, Galilée, 1974).
95. J. Derrida, *Positions*.
96. P. Dews, *The Logics of Disintegration*, p. 70.
97. Ibid., same page.
98. J. Lacan, *Écrits, A Selection*, pp. 40–113.
99. J. Lacan, *Seminaire*, III, p. 223.
100. J. Lacan, *Écrits*, p. 126.
101. J. Lacan, ibid., p. 83.
102. J. Lacan, *Le Seminaire Livre: Les Écrits Techniques de Freud*, Paris, 1975, p. 240.
103. J. Lacan, *Écrits*, p. 40.
104. Ibid., p. 43.
105. Ibid., p. 43.
106. L. Irigaray, *This Sex*, p. 155.
107. Ibid., pp. 155–6.
108. L. Irigaray, *Speculum*, p. 21.
109. L. Irigaray, *This Sex*, p. 80

Chapter 6

1. Louis Althusser, *For Marx*, p. 232.
2. Louis Althusser, 'Ideological State Apparatuses', in *Lenin and Philosophy and Other Essays* (London: NLB, 1971).
3. Ibid., p. 133.
4. Louis Althusser, 'Freud and Lacan', in *Lenin and Philosophy*, p. 189.
5. Ibid., p. 196.
6. Ibid., p. 196.
7. René Descartes, '1st Meditation', in (eds) E. Anscombe and P.T. Geach, *Descartes' Philosophical Writings* (London: Nelson University Paperbacks, 1970), p. 61.
8. René Descartes, '2nd Meditation', in *Descartes Philosophical Writings*, p. 103.
9. J.S. Fichte, *The Science of Knowledge* (Cambridge: CUP, 1982).
10. Louis Althusser, *Ideological State Apparatuses*, p. 168.
11. Ibid., p. 160.

12. Ibid., p. 161.
13. Ibid., pp. 161–2.
14. Ibid., p. 165.
15. Ibid., p. 166.
16. Ibid., p. 166.
17. Ibid., p. 169.
18. Paul Hirst, *On Law and Ideology* (London: Macmillan, 1982).
19. Terry Eagleton, *Literary Theory: An Introduction* (Minneapolis: University of Minnesota Press, 1983).
20. E.P. Thompson, *The Poverty of Theory* (London: Merlin, 1978).
21. Louis Althusser, *Essays in Self Criticism* (London: NLB, 1976), p. 130.
22. Kate Soper, *Humanism and Anti-Humanism* (London: Hutchinson, 1986), p. 108.
23. See, for example, A. Ferguson, *Blood at the Root* (London: Pandora Press, 1989), and Alison Assiter, *Pornography, Feminism and the Individual* (London: Pluto Press, 1989).
24. A. Ferguson, *Blood at the Root*, p. 35.
25. See Gloria Joseph and Jill Lewis, *Common Differences: Conflicts in Black and White Perspectives* (New York: Doubleday, Anchor, 1981).
26. Gayle Rubin, 'The Traffic in Women', in Regina Reiter (ed.) *Towards a New Anthropology of Women* (New York: Monthly Review, 1975).
27. Sigmund Freud, 'Letter to Fliess', No. 71, 15 October 1897 in *Freud's Works*, Vol.1 (London: Hogarth, 1966).
28. Sigmund Freud, *On Sexuality*, p. 316 (London: Penguin, 1977).
29. Ibid., p. 317.
30. See Donzelot.
31. Sigmund Freud, *On Sexuality* (1977), p. 320.
32. Ibid., p. 341.
33. Sigmund Freud, 'A Child is being Beaten', in *On Psychopathology* (London: Pelican, 1983).
34. Sigmund Freud, 'On the Sexual Theories of Young Children' (1908) in Sigmund Freud, *On Sexuality*.
35. Sigmund Freud, *On Sexuality*, p. 193.
36. Janet Sayers, *Biological Politics*.
37. Sigmund Freud, *Totem and Taboo* (1912–1913) (London: Hogarth Press, 1955).
38. Karen Horney, 'The Denial of the Vagina', *International Journal of Psychoanalysis*, 14, 57, 1933.
39. Janet Sayers, *Sexual Contradictions* (London: Tavistock Publications, 1986), p. 38.
40. Karen Horney, 'The Problem of Female Masochism', *Psychoanalytic Review*, 22, 241 (1935).
41. Charles Berhaimer and Claire Kehane (eds), *In Dora's Case: Freud-Hysteria-Feminism* (New York: Columbia University Press 1985).

42. Ibid., p. 145.
43. Toril Moi, *Representations of Patriarchy*, in ibid.
44. Tom Ryan, 'The Roots of Masculinity', in Andrew Metcalf (ed) *The Sexuality of Men* (London: Pluto Press, 1985).
46. D. Kahn et al., 'Sex Role Concepts of 2 and 3 year olds', *Child Development*, No. 49 (1978), pp. 445–51.
47. J. Blakeman et al., 'Sex Appropriate Toy Preference and the Ability to Conceptualise Toys as Sex-Role Related', *Developmental Psychology*, No. 15 (1979), pp. 339–40.
48. See, for example, Philippe Aries, *Centuries of Childhood; A Social History of Family Life* (New York: Random House, 1962); Edward Shorter, *The Making of the Modern Family* (New York: Basic Books, 1975), and Lawrence Stone, *The Family, Sex and Marriage in England, 1500–1800* (London: Weidenfeld and Nicolson, 1977).
49. A. Ferguson, *Blood at the Root*, p. 172.
50. Nawal el Saadawi, *The Hidden Face of Eve* (London: Zed Press, 1969).
51. Giles Deleuze and Felix Guattari, *Anti-Oedipus* (New York: Viking Press, 1977).
52. A. Ferguson, *Blood at the Root*, p. 77.
53. See Valerie Amos and Prathiba Parma, 'Challenging Imperial Feminism', *Feminist Review*, No. 17 (1984).

Bibliography

Works of Louis Althusser

L. Althusser, *For Marx* (Harmondsworth: Penguin, 1969).
——. *Lenin and Philosophy* (London: NLB, 1971).
——. *Essays in Self Criticism* (London: NLB, 1976).
L. Althusser and E. Balibar, *Reading Capital* (London: NLB, 1970).

Other Works

P. Armstrong and H. Armstrong, 'Beyond Sexless Class and Classless Sex', in R. Hamilton and M. Barrett (eds), *The Politics of Diversity* (London: Verso, 1987).

A. Assiter, *Pornography, Feminism and the Individual* (London: Pluto, 1989).

J. Banaji, 'Modes of Production in a Materialist Conception of History', *Capital and Class*, No. 3, 1977.

M. Barrett, *Women's Oppression Today: Problems in Marxist Feminist Analysis* (London: Verso, 1980).

B. Barry, *Political Argument* (Atlantic Highlands, New Jersey: Humanities Press, 1976).

R. Barthes, *Elements of Semiology* (London: Cape Editions, 1967).

S.I. Benn and R.S. Peters, *Social Principles and the Democratic State* (London: Allen and Unwin, 1959).

T. Benton, *Philosophical Foundations of Three Sociologies* (London: Routledge, 1977).
——. *The Rise and Fall of Structural Marxism* (London: Verso, 1984).

R. Bhaskar, *A Realist Philosophy of Science* (Leeds: Leeds Books, 1975).

E. Boulding, *Women in the 20th Century World* (New York and London: Halstead Press, 1977).

E.P. Brandon, 'Reason not the Need', Education for Development, 1980.

D. Braybrooke, 'Let Needs Diminish that Preferences may Prosper', N. Rescher (ed), *Studies in Moral Philosophy* (Oxford: Blackwell, 1968).

A. Callinicos, *Althusser's Marxism* (London: Pluto Press. 1975).

N. Chomsky, 'Knowledge of Language', *Minnesota Studies in the Philosophy of Science* (Minneapolis: University of Minnesota Press, 1975).

G.A. Cohen, *Karl Marx's Theory of History: A Defence* (Oxford: Clarendon Press, 1978).

P. Corrigan, *Socialist Construction and Marxist Theory* (London: Macmillan, 1978).

R. Coward, 'Rethinking Marxism', *m/f*, No. 2, 1978. R. Coward and J. Ellis, *Language and Materialism* (London, Henley and Boston: Routledge, 1977).

D. Davidson and G. Harman (eds), *Semantics of Natural Languages* (Dortrecht: Reidel, 1972).

J. Deleuze and F. Guattari, *Anti-Oedipus* (New York: Viking Press, 1977).

C. Delphy, *The Main Enemy* (London: WRRC, 1977).

J. Derrida, *The Margins of Philosophy* (Brighton: Harvester, 1972).

———. *Of Grammatology* (Baltimore and London: Johns Hopkins University Press, 1976).

———. *Writing and Difference* (London, Henley and Boston: Routledge, 1978).

———. *Positions* (London, 1981).

R. Descartes, 'Meditations', in E.G. Anscombe and P. Geach (eds), *Descartes' Philosophical Writings* (London: Nelson University Paperbacks, 1970).

M. Devitt and K. Sterelny, *Language and Reality: An Introduction to the Philosophy of Language* (Oxford: Blackwell, 1987).

P. Dews, *Logics of Disintegration, Post Structuralist Thought and the Claim of Critical Theory* (London: Verso, 1987).

H. Draper, 'The Dictatorship of the Proletariat', *New Politics*, Vol. 1, No. 4, 1962.

C. Duchen, 'Women's Difference', in *French Connections, Voices from the Women's Movement in France*, trans. Duchen (London: Hutchinson, 1987).

T. Eagleton, *Literary Theory: An Introduction* (Minneapolis: University of Minnesota Press, 1983).

D. Ehrensaft, 'Shared Parenting', *Politics and Power*, No. 3, 1981.

S. Ellenburg, *Rousseau's Political Philosophy: an Interpretation from Within* (New York: Cornell University Press, 1976).

G. Elliot, *Althusser: The Detour of Theory* (London: Verso, 1987).

F. Engels, 'The Origin of the Family, Private Property and the State', in *Marx and Engels, Selected Works in One Volume* (London: Lawrence and Wishart, 1968).

A. Ferguson, *Blood at the Root* (London: Pandora Press, 1989).

P. K. Feyerabend, 'Explanation, Reduction and Empiricism', in *Minnesota Studies in the Philosophy of Science* (Minneapolis: University of Minnesota Press, 1962).

———. 'Against Method', in *Minnesota Studies in the Philosophy of Science*, H. Feigl and S. Maxwell (eds) (Minneapolis: University of Minnesota Press, 1965).

———. 'How to be a Good Empiricist – a Plea for Tolerance in Matters Epistemological', in B.A. Brody (ed), *Readings in the Philosophy of Science* (New Jersey: Prentice Hall, 1970).

———. *Against Method* (London: NLB, 1975).

S. Firestone, *The Dialectic of Sex: the Case for Feminist Revolution* (London: Paladin, 1971).

S. Freud, *Totem and Taboo* (London: Hogarth Press, 1955).

——. *The Interpretation of Dreams* (New York: Avon Books, 1965).

——. *The Standard Edition to the Complete Psychological Works of S. Freud* (London: Hogarth, 1953–74).

——. *On Sexuality* (London: Penguin, 1977).

——. *On Psychopathology* (London: Pelican, 1983).

B. Friedan, *The Feminine Mystique* (New York: Norton, 1963).

J. Gallop, *Feminism and Psychoanalysis* (London: Macmillan, 1982).

N. Geras, *Marx and Human Nature* (London: Verso, 1983).

H. Hartmann, 'The Unhappy Marriage of Marxism and Feminism', *Capital and Class*, No. 8, 1979.

S. W. F. Hegel (see Knox, below).

R. Hilton (ed), *The Transition from Feudalism to Capitalism* (London: NLB, 1976).

S. Hook, *Towards an Understanding of Karl Marx* (London: Gollancz, 1933).

K. Horney, *Feminine Psychology* (New York: Norton, 1967).

L. Irigaray, *Speculum of the Other Woman* (New York: Cornell University Press, 1985).

——. *This Sex which is not One* (New York: Cornell University Press, 1985).

R. Johnson, 'Edward Thompson, Eugene Genovese and Socialist Humanist History', *History Workshop*, No. 6, Autumn, 1978.

C. Joll, 'Teacher's Pay', quoted in the Bristol Women's Studies Group (eds), *Half the Sky* (London: Virago, 1979).

R. Keat and J. Urry, *Social Theory as Science* (London, Henley and Boston: Routledge, 1975).

T.M. Knox (trans.), *Hegel's Philosophy of Right* (London, Oxford, New York: Oxford University Press, 1980).

J. Koethe, 'Putnam's Argument Against Realism', *Philosophical Review*, 1979.

T. Kuhn, *The Structure of Scientific Revolutions* (Chicago: Chicago University Press, 1970).

J. Lacan, *Écrits: A Selection*, trans. A. Sheridan (London: Tavistock, 1977).

C. Lévi-Strauss, *Structural Anthropology* (New York, London: Basic Books, 1963).

J. Lloyd, *The Man of Reason* (London: Methuen, 1984).

A. Macyntre, 'Spinoza', *The Encyclopaedia of Philosophy* (London and New York: Macmillan and The Free Press, 1967).

C. McGinn, 'A Note on the Essence of Natural Kinds', *Analysis* 35, 1974–5.

M. McIntosh, 'Gender and Economics: The Sexual Division of Labour and the Subordination of Women' in *Of Marriage and the Market* (London: CSE Books, 1981).

K. Marx, *Misère de la Philosophie* (Paris: Verlag, 1908).

——. *The German Ideology* (London: Lawrence and Wishart, 1965).

——. *Selected Works in One Volume* (London: Lawrence and Wishart, 1968).

——. *Theories of Surplus Value*, Part 1 (Moscow: Progress Publishers, 1969).

——. *Capital*, Volume 3 (London: Lawrence and Wishart, 1971).

——. *Grundrisse* (Harmondsworth: Penguin Books, 1973).

———. *Capital*, Volume 1, trans. Ben Fowkes (Harmondsworth: Penguin and NLB, 1976).

K. Marx and F. Engels, *Werke*, Vol. XVIII (Berlin: Institut für Marxismus-Leninismus beim 2K der SED, Dietz Verlag, 1964).

K. Marx and F. Engels, *Selected Works*, Three Volumes (Moscow: Progress Publishers, 1969).

K. Marx and F. Engels, *Selected Correspondence* (Moscow: Progress Publishers, 1975).

M. Mead, *Sex and Temperament in Three Primitive Societies* (London: Routledge, 1935).

———. *Male and Female: A Study of the Sexes in a Changing World* (Harmondsworth: Penguin, 1962).

D. Miller, *Social Justice* (Oxford: Clarendon Press, 1976).

R.W. Miller, 'Productive Forces and the Forces of Change: A Review of G.A. Cohen's *Karl Marx's Theory of History: A Defence*', *Philosophical Review*, January 1981.

T. Moi, *Sexual-Textual Politics* (London: Methuen, 1985).

A. Naess, *Freedom, Emotion and Self-Subsistence* (Oslo: Universitats Verloget, 1975).

A. Nye, *Feminist Theory and the Philosophies of Man* (London: Croom Helm, 1988).

A. Oakley, *Sex, Gender and Society* (London: Maurice Temple Smith Ltd, 1972).

A. Phillips, 'Marxism and Feminism', *Revolutionary Feminism*, No. 6, Winter 1980, pp. 145–7.

———. *Divided Loyalties, Dilemmas of Sex and Class* (London: Virago, 1987).

S.V. Plekhanov, *Fundamental Problems of Marxism* (London, 1908).

A. Pollert, *Girls, Wives, Factory Lives* (London: Pluto Press, 1981).

N. Poulantzas, *Political Power and Social Classes* (London: NLB and Sheed and Ward, 1973).

H. Putman, *Mind, Language and Reality* (Cambridge: Cambridge University Press, 1975).

———. *Meaning and the Moral Sciences* (London: Routledge, 1978).

J. Richards, *The Sceptical Feminist* (London: Routledge, 1980).

R. Rohlich-Leavitt, *Women, Cross Culturally, Change and Challenge* (The Hague, Paris: Mouton Publishers, 1975).

A. Rossi (ed), *The Feminist Papers* (New York and London: Columbia University Press, 1973).

J.J. Rousseau, *The Social Contract and Discourses* (London: Dent, 1968).

———. *The Confessions* (London: Penguin, 1984).

S. Rowbotham, *Hidden from History* (London: Pluto Press, 1974).

M. Ryan, *Marxism and Deconstruction* (Baltimore: Johns Hopkins University Press, 1982).

J. Sayers, *Biological Politics* (London: Tavistock, 1982).

———. *Sexual Contradictions* (London: Tavistock, 1986).

——. 'Forces of Production and Relations of Production in Socialist Society', *Radical Philosophy*, No. 24, Spring 1980.

F. de Saussure, *Course in General Linguistics* (C. Bally and A. Sechehaye, eds) in collaboration with A. Riedlinger (New York, Toronto London: McGraw Hill Book Co, 1966).

——. 'Course in General Linguistics' in R. and F. George (eds), *The Structuralists from Marx to Lévi-Strauss* (Garden City, New York: Anchor Books, 1972).

A. Schaff, *Structuralism and Marxism* (Oxford, New York, Sydney, Toronto: Pergamon Press, 1978).

L. Segal, *Is the Future Female?* (London: Virago, 1987).

L. Seve, *Man in Marxist Theory and the Psychology of the Personality* (trans. J. Mcgreal) (Brighton: Harvester, 1978).

W. Shaw, *Marx's Theory of History* (Stanford: Stanford University Press, 1978).

T. Skillen, 'Post Marxist Modes of Production', *Radical Philosophy*, No. 20, Summer 1978.

K. Soper, 'On Materialisms', *Radical Philosophy*, No. 15, 1976.

——. *Humanism and Anti-Humanism* (London: Hutchinson, 1986).

C. Sumner, *Reading Ideologies, an Investigation into the Marxist Theory of Ideology and Law* (London, New York, San Francisco: Academic Press, 1979).

E.P. Thompson, *The Poverty of Theory and Other Essays* (London: Merlin Press, 1979).

S. Timpanaro, *On Materialism* (London: NLB, 1975).

Y.N. Vološinov, *Freudianism: A Marxist Critique* (New York: Academic Press, 1976).

J. Wild, *Spinoza: Selections* (New York, Chicago, Boston: Charles Scribner's Sons, 1930).

Index